'Written by one of our most lucid and erudite psychoanalytic writers, Barnaby Barratt's *Free Association* is here to remind us what psychoanalysis is really about. This short – but mighty! – book walks the reader through the forgotten, if not repressed, art of free-association. Making a powerful case against the degradation of psychoanalysis into a narratological project of self-discovery, *Free Association* demonstrates how critical it is for our discipline to think and *feel* with psychic energy. Barratt's book is the introductory class to a mode of psychoanalysis that so many psychoanalysts miss!'

Avgi Saketopoulu, *psychoanalyst and author of* Sexuality beyond Consent

'Since his 1984 *Psychic Reality and Psychoanalytic Knowing*, Dr Barnaby B Barratt has made a significant impact on the field of psychoanalysis. As a rare clinician-theorist, his onto-ethical psychoanalysis, with his revisioning of Freud's free-association as a 'radicalized' practice, positions Barratt – similar to psychoanalytic mystics such as Michael Eigen – as a leading-edge elder, ensuring an ever-deepening of the long-forgotten promise of psychoanalysis: the 'voicing' of repressed energies. Barratt's work continues to inspire, broaden, and challenge the field, recovering its onto-ethical seriousness for the next generation.'

Loray Daws, PhD, DPsa, *psychoanalyst and author of* Michael Eigen.

"Barratt's essay is an impressive and original examination of a topic essential to the distinctiveness of psychoanalysis. The thoughtful reader will gain much.'

Dr Jonathan Sklar, FRCPsych, *Independent Training Analyst, British Psychoanalytic Society.*

'Barnaby B. Barratt's writings are a psychoanalytic treasure trove. Old ideas, dusted off and reappraised, gain new meaning, transforming seemingly fixed matter into raw energy by the mere act of reading his work. By resurrecting Freud's now atrophied notions of psychic energy and asserting the primacy of free-association,

Barratt articulates and brings alive a sensuous, sensational erotics and ethics of psychoanalysis urgently relevant to today's human, global, and planetary predicaments and thus to our future.'

Jill Gentile, PhD, *psychoanalyst and author of* Feminine Law.

'I wish I had begun reading Barratt's writings in 1984 when he published his first book on psychoanalysis and its philosophy. I would have lived a different life, but I only discovered him in my late 50s. He revitalized my psychoanalytic thinking and practice, setting me forth on new paths of intellectual and spiritual adventure. I hope this book introduces many readers, especially students, to this titan of Western thought, Eastern spirit, and psychoanalysis.'

Dr Philip Lance, *Faculty at the Southern California University of Health Sciences, and with the Psychoanalytic Center of California.*

'Barnaby Barratt is one of the most original and rigorous thinkers in psychoanalysis today. In continuing to advance his legacy, he provides a concise inquiry, critique, and reinterpretation, not only of the free-associative method, but of psychoanalysis itself. Another master course by a brilliant psychoanalyst.'

Professor Jon Mills, *psychoanalyst and author of* End of the World.

Free Association

In *Free Association: A Contemporary Introduction*, Barnaby Barratt presents a compelling and much-needed exploration of the method of free association within psychoanalytic treatment.

This concise yet comprehensive book examines the historical roots, philosophical implications, and transformative impact on the human psyche of free association, making it an essential resource for understanding the deep unconscious forces that shape our lives. Barratt demonstrates how free association uniquely reveals dimensions of the human condition that remain hidden in ordinary therapeutic approaches. Readers will gain insight into the distinctions between psychoanalysis and psychotherapy, the significance of repression and psychic energy, and the profound shifts in being that free association facilitates. Barratt's critical analysis of prevailing theories and alternative methods, such as somatic and shamanic practices, highlights the unparalleled ability of free association to reinvigorate psychic energies and existential freedom.

This book is a vital resource for psychoanalysts in training and practice, and anyone deeply curious about the human psyche. It is also a valuable tool for instructors and researchers in psychoanalysis, psychotherapy, and related fields.

Barnaby B Barratt is a research and training psychoanalyst in Johannesburg and Cape Town, South Africa. He is a Director of the Institute for Rediscovering Psychoanalysis, and was previously Professor of Family Medicine, Psychiatry and Behavioural Neurosciences at Wayne State University in Detroit, USA. He is the author of *Beyond Psychotherapy: On Becoming a (Radical) Psychoanalyst* (2019), *Radical Psychoanalysis: An Essay on Free-Associative Praxis* (2016) and *What is Psychoanalysis?: 100 Years after Freud's 'Secret Committee'* (2013).

Free Association

A Contemporary Introduction

Barnaby B Barratt

Routledge
Taylor & Francis Group
LONDON AND NEW YORK

Designed cover image: © Michal Heiman, Asylum 1855–2020, The Sleeper (video, psychoanalytic sofa and Plate 34), exhibition view, Herzliya Museum of Contemporary Art, 2017

First published 2026
by Routledge
4 Park Square, Milton Park, Abingdon, Oxon OX14 4RN

and by Routledge
605 Third Avenue, New York, NY 10158

Routledge is an imprint of the Taylor & Francis Group, an informa business

British Library Cataloguing-in-Publication Data
A catalogue record for this book is available from the British Library

Library of Congress Cataloging-in-Publication Data
A catalog record has been requested for this book

ISBN: 978-1-032-90483-2 (hbk)
ISBN: 978-1-032-90481-8 (pbk)
ISBN: 978-1-003-55826-2 (ebk)

DOI: 10.4324/9781003558262

Typeset in Times New Roman
by Taylor & Francis Books

Access the [Instructor and Student Resources/Support Material]:
[insert ISR/ Support Material URL]

May all beings be happy and free;
may these writings contribute
to the happiness and freedom of all beings.

Contents

Series Editor's Preface

Routledge Introductions to Contemporary Psychoanalysis is one of the most prominent psychoanalytic publishing ventures of our day. The series' aim is to become an encyclopedia of psychoanalysis, with each entry given its own book.

This comprehensive series illuminates the intricate landscape of psychoanalytic theory and practice. In this collection of concise yet illuminating volumes, we delve into the influential figures, groundbreaking concepts, and transformative theories that shape the contemporary psychoanalytic landscape.

At the heart of each volume lies a commitment to clarity, accessibility, and depth. Our expert authors, renowned scholars and practitioners in their respective fields, guide readers through the complexities of psychoanalytic thought with precision and enthusiasm. Whether you are a seasoned psychoanalyst, a student eager to explore the field, or a curious reader seeking insight into the human psyche, our series offers a wealth of knowledge and insight.

Each volume serves as a gateway into a specific aspect of psychoanalytic theory and practice. From the pioneering works of Sigmund Freud to the innovative contributions of modern theorists such as Antonino Ferro and Michal Eigen, our series covers a diverse range of topics, including seminal figures, key concepts, and emerging trends. Whether you are interested in classical psychoanalysis, object relations theory, or the intersection of neuroscience and psychoanalysis, you will find a wealth of resources within our collection.

One of the hallmarks of our series is its interdisciplinary approach. While rooted in psychoanalytic theory, our volumes draw upon insights from psychology, philosophy, sociology, and other disciplines to offer a holistic understanding of the human mind and its complexities.

Each volume in the series is crafted with the reader in mind, balancing scholarly rigor with engaging prose. Whether you are embarking on your journey into psychoanalysis or seeking to deepen your understanding of specific topics, our series provides a clear and comprehensive roadmap.

Moreover, our series is committed to fostering dialogue and debate within the psychoanalytic community. Each volume invites readers to critically engage with the material, encouraging reflection, discussion, and further exploration.

We invite you to join us on this journey of discovery as we explore the ever-evolving landscape of psychoanalysis.

Aner Govrin

Psychoanalytic books by Barnaby B Barratt

Psychic Reality and Psychoanalytic Knowing (1984/2016)

Psychoanalysis and the Postmodern Impulse (1993/2016)

The Emergence of Somatic Psychology and Bodymind Therapy (2010)

What is Psychoanalysis? 100 Years after Freud's 'Secret Committee' (2013)

Radical Psychoanalysis: An Essay on Free-associative Praxis (2016)

Beyond Psychotherapy: On Becoming a (Radical) Psychoanalyst (2019)

Prefatory note: Forgotten essential of psycho-*analysis*?

Not unlike the notion of freedom, 'free-association' is a term for the expressiveness of our psyche that is coined quite frequently yet rarely understood. Leaving aside whatever legal or political meanings the term may have, one cannot even begin to introduce the notion of free-association—let alone appreciate its extensive and intensive power to shake up our psyche beneficially—without some contextual grasp of the entire history of a discipline called 'psychoanalysis.'

This is because, on the one side, there are practitioners who hold—as I do—that there is no psychoanalysis unless this method of the human subject's expressing itself is prioritized as essential, both ethically and ontologically. These psychoanalysts, who are a small minority of those who give themselves this title, understand free-association as a praxis that is the heart and soul of the revolutionary processes of changeful inquiry that were initiated by Sigmund Freud (1856–1939). Yet, on the other side, it is merely a technique that has been—in the minds of so many professionals who refer to themselves as 'psychoanalysts'—superseded by a variety of other psychotherapeutic practices. At best it is held to be some sort of epistemological adjunct to whatever they call 'psychoanalysis. Thus it is demoted to being just one among many modes of access to a certain type of information that can be used to manipulate change interpretively, which is a procedure of psychotherapy.

In short, one cannot begin to introduce and appreciate free-association without some grasp of all that has happened to this multifarious discipline in the century subsequent to the two decades of its inception, which was between 1895 and 1914. So, the challenge of writing a 'contemporary introduction' to free-association is not only to offer an exposition of this method of discourse as essential to an authentic praxis of psychoanalysis. It is also to explain how and why it is that the uniqueness of its significance as a method or praxis seems almost to have been forgotten. That is, to ask what has happened—and why—to the discipline that was birthed by the praxis or method of free-association, such that the mainstream of this discipline has progressively sidelined, or even repudiated, the very method that Freud said was essential to its conduct.

Free-association has been demoted and disregarded in the course of the past century, and I think it is fair to assert that the character and conditions of its discourse have never been all that well understood. So, unlike many topics that have been introduced with studious even-handedness, this essay offers a way of understanding free-association that is maverick. An ordinary introduction—with a comprehensive examination of the extant literature, such as is required in the opening chapters of every doctoral dissertation—cannot do justice to the confusion and contumacy that surrounds this particular topic. In large measure, this is because the controversies that underlie the relevant issues have rarely been debated openly. Consequently, much of the professional literature is based on what I will show to be mistaken assumptions about the significance of this method as praxis, and indeed mistaken assumptions about the discipline, which is defined by its engagement. Thus, in a way that is not immediately obvious from a reading of the literature, the notion of free-association is actually at the crux of a philosophical controversy about what sort of a discipline 'psychoanalysis' might be. This is the case even when the discipline is restrictively defined as an unusual sort of dialogue between a practitioner and an adult patient (nothing about work with children or groups will be addressed herein). What sort of processes—free-associative or not—are at work and at play in this discourse?

The prevailing—metaphysical and metapsychological—standpoint is that psychoanalysis is fundamentally a practice of *knowing about* something, even if the thing 'known about' is identical with the personage of the knower. Knowing about oneself, knowing about the patient, knowing about the unconscious (whatever this 'unconscious' may mean). The threefold implication is (i) that there is a knower separate from the something known, even when the known is the self, (ii) that the knowledge accruing to this entity's experience is representational (interpretations, insights, formulations), and (iii) that this knowledge, when applied, causes or propels whatever experiential changes, in the knower and/or the known, may result from this procedure. This is the nub of instrumental reason or agential rationality. Of course, there is an affiliated view, accompanied by a somewhat bloated literature, that emphasizes how necessary are the emotional and relational contexts within which this production of new knowledge and experience may occur.

This is the literature on transference, on fantasies of 'new' relationships (and on the disconfirmation of such transferences), even on the imputed phenomena of 're-parenting' and so forth. But the *epistemological* emphasis is still pervasive and fundamental. 'Psychoanalysis' is supposed to conform to the primacy and priority of knowing, within the traditional binarism of the knower and the thing known (even when the latter causes a reflective reconstitution of the former). It is the expansion of representation, notably self-representation, that counts. The discipline concerns what can be known about—represented by—the functioning of our psyche, and how this epistemological advance drives changes in the knower and/or the known. This has been the majority standpoint which inscribes several metaphysical assumptions.

As will be presented herein, there is a radically divergent standpoint by which both to appreciate the processes of psychoanalysis and to understand the unique power of its free-associative praxis. This values free-association as signifying a methodical break with the euromodern masterdiscourse (which will be defined and critiqued in the course of this essay). This metaphysical masterdiscourse assumes the primacy and priority of epistemics; knowing something about something comes first. Against this metaphysical stance, the divergent appreciation of psychoanalysis turns to the ground of ontology, which emphasizes the issues of being and becoming, and to ethical discourse, which is the praxis of opening to what *is*—that is, opening to whatever becomes, rather than trying to capture it and tie it down, judgmentally and moralistically, in an epistemological formulation. Thus, the discourse of each treatment session is not to be appreciated and understood in terms of the appearances of epistemological advance but as foremost and fundamentally a renewed movement in the being-becoming of what *is*, an opening of discourse to that which the knower has suppressed or repressed.

It must be quickly emphasized that this is *not* merely an emotional and relational process (as in ideas of transference cure, reparenting, and so on), *nor* is it simply the restart of a preprogrammed developmental progression that had been arrested by trauma. Rather, against the primacy and priority of epistemology, psychoanalytic praxis is an *ontoethical* process— achievable by a commitment to free-associative discourse. In this process, the knowledge of the knower is unsettled, deconstructed or interrogated in a negative dialectic, so that the being-becoming of the subject can be remobilized, as the obstructions—inhibitions or contortions—inscribed in the presumptions of representational knowledge are moved aside, dissolved, or bracketed-off.

This is psycho-*analysis*. The term 'analysis'—labelling the discipline—has all too frequently been misunderstood as referring to a logical deductive or inductive procedure, a calculus by which interpretations of 'what's what' are generated. This error has bedevilled the history of the discipline. In 1919, Freud told an audience that in his discipline *analysis* means breaking up or separating out, and suggests an analogy with the labour of chemists on compounds they find in nature and analyse in their laboratories. Against Carl Jung, he argued strenuously that so-called psycho-*synthesis*—which had been promulgated by Robert Assagioli and which Freud dismissed as a 'thoughtless term'–was *not* the task of the psychoanalyst. Rather, any synthesis should be left to patients, who are free to put together whatever they experience psychoanalytically in whatever way they wish.

The point here is that the changeful power of the discipline is not to be considered in terms of the production and application of new knowledge (insights, interpretations, formulations). Rather, change in our being-becoming arises from unsettling the knowledge of the knower—that is, deconstructing the repetitiously-compulsive way in which such 'knowledge' has impeded the movement of being-becoming. This is a minority standpoint as to the significance of Freud's discoveries. However, I believe it must be seriously entertained—we will find it central to an understanding of the contentious character of the notion of free-association.

All this—unfamiliar and densely intimated as it may be in these prefatory notes—makes a new discussion of free-associative discourse both timely and critical. This is because how one appreciates and understands free-association—whether as epistemological technique or ontoethical praxis—is pivotal to our fundamental comprehension of the discipline as a whole. This essay introduces the notion of free-association in a way that explicates and re-instates its unique status because any significant discussion of free-associative processes compels us to decide, as it were, between the competing standpoints intimated above (which are to be elaborated in this essay).

An 'introduction' to free-association cannot sidestep these issues, which should not be disregarded or trivialized as 'too philosophical' and certainly cannot be regarded as clinically irrelevant. Many readers, reviewers, and critics may well complain that in the course of this essay I not only introduce the method of free-association but effectively redefine the discipline we call psychoanalysis. If that is the case, I would counter that this does not warrant apology.

BBB / April 2025
Johannesburg and Cape Town, South Africa

[illegible]

Chapter 1

On expressing oneself

The polyglot discipline called 'psychoanalysis' has been embroiled in much brouhaha, controversy, and commotion, from its inception with Freud's clinical labours in the final years of the 19th century, and still today. Perhaps one of the few propositions that are generally agreed is that it is a mode of healing. According to its proponents, it is indeed a profound practice of healing. According to its opponents, it isn't, although they generally concede that it is intended to be. They think its claims are bogus and–for much of what calls itself 'psychoanalysis' today—perhaps they are right.[1] But those of us who have achieved the privilege of authentically entering into an intense process of free-association in the listening presence of a genuinely qualified and devoted psychoanalyst know well the uniquely healing properties of this method. So, we should start this essay with a question: What do we mean by healing? More particularly, what do we mean by *healing the psyche*, with all the suffering that it endures?

Let us provisionally define 'psyche' in a limited manner. Of course, we must be aware that the term derives from the Greek *psykhe* (or the older *psychein*), connoting not only mind but also breath, spirit, and the liveliness of life. We will explore the significance of this later (indeed, by the end of this essay a very wide and wild definition of the notion of psyche will have been introduced and discussed). But at this juncture, a definition, which is more or less consistent with the secular emergence of Euro-American psychology in the modern era, delimits the psyche to the mind as our entire system of thoughts, feelings, wishes, and

DOI: 10.4324/9781003558262-1

fantasies. That is, our *inner theatre of representations* about our self, about others, about things, about the world in general, and about our affects and actions in relation to all these. Whether in imagistic, linguistic, or enactive constructions, psychology encompasses our lived-experiences to the extent that we can represent them in these modalities. Later we will consider movements of psychic energy as an unrepresentable dimension of our lived-experience, but for now let us hold to the narrow dogma that if it cannot be represented, it cannot be considered an aspect of our psyche; despite the possibility that it can—in a sense to be discussed later—be experienced. The psyche, as a personalized representational system, inevitably involves conflict and contradiction. To a greater or lesser extent and in various ways, our psyche confronts its own suffering from the cradle to the grave (we will also postpone for later discussion why this is so).

What does it mean to heal an individual's inner theatre of representations? What is implied when some authority declares that this or that individual's system of re-presentationally experiencing self and world is 'broken' and needs 'fixing'? The notion of healing is not unproblematic, especially since it is framed and generated by our considerable human capacity for fantasy. So, we should begin this essay by briefly considering such questions.

There is a sense in which our psyche continuously strives to mend itself, even if unsuccessfully (that is, even when it never achieves the success it fantasizes is possible). As humans, we are, whether we realize it or not, almost constantly seeking—desiring, or thinking about—ways to heal. To make ourselves *feel* better, more integrated, more whole. Here I emphasize the issue of feeling whole because often—as psychoanalysis so resolutely demonstrates—we feel most integrated precisely when we are not. Conflict and contradiction are integral to the functioning of our psyche. Although sometimes framed as futuristic fantasy—a utopian condition of our being—more often than not our own healing is self-theorized in terms of reversion. That is, we think of it as a 'return' to a harmonious state in which—so we typically believe—we once resided or could have resided. It is as if we believe in the possibility—past or future—of a state of absolute euphony or internal concord, for which there is little or no present evidence. These efforts at healing may be mundane or exotic, profane or sacred, modest or audacious, immanent or transcendent. A good night's sleep, a nutritious meal, a restful vacation, more fulfilling work with appropriate reward, a deep and exciting connection with a new lover, fulfilment of a cherished ideal or vision, prayerful connection with a dimension that is divine, and so on. These are the means by which we believe we will alleviate or even resolve the struggles, conflicts, tensions, traumas—the sources of dissension, anguish, and torment—that we harbour within ourselves. They are ways by which we believe we might return to a 'healthy' state of harmony that perhaps only manifests itself as an ultimacy in our collective and personal myths as well as in our dreams.

If the positivity of notions such as 'health' and 'return to health' has an inherently mythic or fantasy-imbued quality (the exemplar of which, *par excellence*, is our diverse beliefs about an afterlife), then perhaps it is more realistic to define healing in terms of what it is not. That is, to define what healing cannot be, *if* it is to be authentic (and not some seductive but fraudulent or specious solution). Three tenets are relevant here, and they must be kept in focus if we are to understand why—authentic—psychoanalysis can be such a powerful mode of healing.

Healing is not the avoidance of pain. Today's world of globalized capitalism surrounds us with counterfeit promises of easy healing. The contemporary marketplace is full of products that hold out the hope of personal growth (and easement) without pain: Tablets that will dispel anxieties and disturbing thoughts; programs that will supposedly propel us into a state of self-mastery with almost endless accomplishment; subscriptions to religious, political, and ethnic or tribal organizations; potions and prayers that will repel all things negative; myriad treatments that are intended to evoke our sense of connection with a divine dimension of life, impelling us towards unbounded feelings of bliss or even everlasting ecstasy. And so on.

We live in what the 20th-century philosopher Leszek Kolakowski and others have described as the culture of analgesics, with its commonplace insistence that pain—and even the pain of inescapable loss—can and should be avoided. As one wise colleague said to me 'the promise of more or less effortless self-improvement is the snake-oil of the 20th and 21st centuries.' An analgesic culture promotes a general failure to recognize the meaning of pain, instead advocating its immediate alleviation. It thus denies how pain is intrinsic to the processes of life itself and to what I will call the *lifefulness of healing*. At the very least, the movement of life entails loss, which almost invariably touches us painfully. Instead of accepting and confronting this reality, our analgesic culture commends the concealment of all that is painful, thus ensconcing us in multifarious lifestyles of 'narcotization' supported by manifestoes for promissory futures. What results is an almost anesthetized version of 'living'—the prospects of zombie culture, as some contemporary pundits have characterized it. Against the ideology of pain avoidance, a genuine healing process surely cannot endorse any tendency to avoid confrontation with that which is painful. Personal growth requires the acceptance (and the use) of pain if authentic healing is to occur.

Healing is not the avoidance of death. In Judeo-Christian-Islamic cultures and in some others, it has been traditional to think of death simply as the opposite of life. My own death is, as Freud asserted, intrinsically unthinkable. As soon as I contemplate 'my death'—albeit in my imagination—I am still affirming a 'me' in this present. However, I can think, extrinsically, about the death of others, which in concrete terms means that their lives become absent to me, and I can then try to imagine how such an eventuality might pertain to 'me.' In the aftermath of Freud's sublime but problematically interpreted monograph of 1920, *Beyond the Pleasure Principle*, it is necessary for us to go beyond the conceptual opposition of life/death (why so many interpretations of Freud's essay are problematic must be addressed elsewhere). The theme of life-death's complicity has been taken up subsequently by several brilliant philosophers from Maurice Blanchot, Georges Bataille, and Jacques Derrida to Simon Critchley. In brief, following insights articulated by Sabrina Spielrein in 1912, Freud attempted to articulate the deathfulness that inheres to life itself (at least that is how I think his essay should be read). Every moment, in which our energies crystallize or congeal into meaningfulness—as 'life'—requires the 'death' of other immanent meanings. That is, the abrogation or extinction—abolition or annihilation—of other possibilities. Every creative congregation depends upon dissolution and dispersal of something else, effectively its destruction or self-destruction. Thus, an authentic healing process cannot involve any denial of this inherent and esoteric dimension that I will label—modifying Freud's terminology, but more or less following the thinking of Jean Laplanche and others—the deathfulness that inheres to the liveliness of life itself.

Healing is not a procedure of adaptation. Here I use the concept of 'adaptation' not so much in the biological-evolutionary sense, but more to refer to the individual's adaptation or adjustment to an external sociocultural reality (that is more or less treated as immutable). Especially with the development of psychotherapies in 20th-century Euro-American cultures, all too often the notion of psychological healing has been equated with being 'well adjusted' to current social norms and cultural structures. That there are persons who are 'model citizens,' seemingly content and knowing their place in the sociocultural and political-economic order—as if conforming effortlessly and indeed thriving on the exploitation of those lower in the order—should *not* be taken to imply that they are not in need of healing. Against the idolization of adaptivity, even if one is the capping stone that tops the wall, genuine healing surely cannot amount to living one's life as the proverbial 'brick in the wall' of systemic and structural contexts that are alienating and oppressive. In relation to our mental functioning, counselling and coaching (as well as much that passes for 'psychotherapy') seem to aim at normalizing the individual's lived-experience. That is, aligning the subject's thoughts, feelings, and actions with normative cultural standards. All too often, this makes such professionals the purveyors of prevailing ideology, trading in interpretations that put this subject in its place. They are the contemporary practitioners of those who make their livelihood from the formation and perpetuation of the illusions of the ruling-class or dominant sociopolitical and epistemological order (as Marx discussed in *The German Ideology*). 'Normality' is a notion of which we must be suspicious.

The protocols of healing surely cannot be authentically rallied by slogans such as 'let's get rid of pain, let's deny death, and let's follow the crowd.' Rather, any truthful and liberatory healing of the psyche is launched with questions such as 'Who am I? What am I? and Where am I?' Whether such questions are explicitly articulated or left implicit (and how they bring together past, present, and future), healing the psyche is always both existential or spiritual, and cultural or sociopolitical, in its implications or ramifications. It does not dodge pain nor deny the deathfulness of life itself, and it should not be expected to result in 'model citizens' with bourgeois values that are adjusted to the promulgation and perpetuation of a barbaric world. This must be kept in focus as we proceed because free-association, as the singular method of psychoanalysis, comprises a unique process of listening to the possibilities of response to such questions as Who? What? Where?

The perhaps unsurprising upshot of these preliminary considerations about the notion of healing is that healing requires the holistic expressiveness of that which calls for healing. Addressing some parts of the whole in a manner that is deleterious to other parts surely cannot be considered an authentic mode of healing. As for the necessity of expressiveness, even the broken bone must speak before it can be put in a cast to allow it to mend itself. But what does it mean for the psyche to express itself? For individuals to give voice to their truthfulness? Or to articulate the sources of their suffering? The issue is far more complex than might be anticipated, for it goes not only to the problem of defining 'oneself' but also to the frame in which we conceive the human condition. Freud's so-called 'discovery of the unconscious' is greatly responsible for this conceptual complexification.

Let us start by considering the 'oneself' of our psyche. I can readily articulate the thoughts that are within the purview of my reflective self-consciousness: 'I am thinking about this book.' Self-consciousness is like an 'I-Now-Is' attached to representations that are on the surface of the psyche; 'I am here-and-now existing as a reader of this book.' Innumerable other thoughts can be brought into consciousness and articulated. Unless I am dumbstruck, I can articulate this representation to my neighbour: 'Please don't disturb me, I am reading a book.' I can also hide my thoughts from her. I can lie, and I can be hypocritical: 'I am not reading this book, and you are welcome to disturb me.' When it entails the voicing of secret thoughts and private feelings, the perennial challenge of 'speaking one's own truthfulness' is all too familiar. We all harbour fantasies and opinions that we sequester from the external world (as well as those we secrete from ourselves). In the Euro-American tradition, the question of internality and the twin problems of privacy and self-misrepresentation have been discussed since pre-Socratic philosophy. Misrepresentation, that is, not only to others but even more so to oneself in acts of deliberate imposture or unwitting self-deception. The discipline of psychoanalysis has amplified this discussion immeasurably, specifically in the theorization of what are called 'defence mechanisms.' These operations can be loosely defined as acts in which one—partially—conceals one's own thoughts and feelings from one's own reflective self-consciousness. Of course, this raises philosophical questions about intentionality and authenticity, for which psychoanalysis has been the target of existentialist critique—notably in Jean-Paul Sartre's 1943 opus, *Being and Nothingness.*

Defensive operations are permutations and combinations (displacements and condensations, metonyms and metaphors) of our thinking and feeling whereby we know but, at the same time, do not know what we are keeping secret, not just from others but also from ourselves. To give a commonplace but minacious example of such psychodynamics: The ostensibly heterosexual man who hates gays, slandering them and committing violence against them, is always found (upon psychoanalytic scrutiny) to be 'lying' to himself. He does not know consciously how gay he is, but he knows that he abhors men who seem comfortable with their gayness (subjecting them to his jealous or envious attack). Eventually, through procedures or life changes that we can call psychotherapeutic, he might come to own and to enjoy his own homosexual inclinations and impulses (or he may never be privileged with such personal growth). But in his homophobic fervour (which is girded by the ideology of a heterosexist sociocultural system), he is 'lying' to himself in the sense that he trenchantly denies and suppresses the homoerotic feelings that are, in a recondite sense, active within him. He re-attributes them to others against whom he then rages with loathing. This does not imply that his hatred is unreal or phony. It is what it is. But it also serves to conceal other more conflictual feelings and thoughts that are represented within his psyche but not within the purview of his reflective self-consciousness (the purview of 'I-Now-Is'). They are descriptively unconscious. Such psychodynamic operations can loosely be categorized as diverse acts of suppression (Freud's *Unterdrückung*). Generically, this is what has happened to thoughts and feelings that are still operative and represented (or representable) within the individual's psyche yet are seemingly too dangerous to be allowed into the individual's self-conscious purview.

We have innumerable representations of our lived-experience that have somehow been exiled from the purview of immediacy and are 'descriptively unconscious.' Later in this essay, we will discuss how the manifold modes of suppression differ from the unconscious as formed by repression (Freud's *Verdrängung*). Suppressed ideas may merely have succumbed to 'selective inattention' (as Harry Stack Sullivan called it) or they may be more incisively unacceptable to our sense of self, and thence pressed into a deeper mode of exile. In short, there are 'lightweight' suppressions and there are those that are encoded far more obscurely from our self-reflective purview (but nevertheless remain encoded in some latent sense). With the latter, it is *as if* such representations have been buried in some nether region of the mind, from whence they may or may not ever be excavated (like a traumatic memory that needs to be forgotten but can never actually be representationally expunged). Several psychotherapeutic procedures (that have been derived from Freud's theorizing) aim to bring into reflective self-consciousness those representations that the patient has held at bay by means of defence mechanisms. My point here is that the act of 'giving voice to one's truthfulness' is always more contradictorily complicated than—for example—my simply telling you something that I know well but have kept to myself. Perhaps we should add that the act of truth-telling is nonetheless inherently scary.

Psychoanalysis has made the issue even more complex, and the next few sections may be challenging to grasp, but they are crucial to an understanding of the problematics of 'oneself.' This is because psychoanalysis, and some allied disciplines of the 20th century, have called into question the sense of itself that the 'I' has—namely, a strong sense of belief that it is author of its own thoughts.

Let us suppose that I say, 'this wall is painted indigo,' and then my neighbour says, 'no, it's violet' (we might merely be using different colour labels, but then again one cannot discount the possibility that we are actually seeing different colours). However, it is comparatively clear that the representation of a violet wall belongs to her and that of an indigo wall belongs to me. Yet this cannot be taken to imply that either of us authored these representations (even if we are, in a sociocultural sense, the authority on what are our own opinions). Psychoanalysis calls into question what it means for a representation to 'belong' to anyone. Beyond the platitude that 'I have my thoughts, and she has hers,' matters become complicated. All these representations, and our ability to exchange them conversationally, depend on the rules and regulations of what Ludwig Wittgenstein called 'language-games' (or, similarly, of what John Austin would later call 'speech-acts'). My neighbour and I both operate within the system and structure of such games. We are adept at it, and indeed we have the—almost entirely spurious—sense that we are in charge of their operation. That is, we all are under the illusion that—and we experience ourselves *as if*—the author of 'my own' thoughts and feelings is 'I.' The problematic issue is threefold.

First: Contrary to what we tend to believe, the representational 'I' of lived-experience—what we call the 'subject' from an internal standpoint, or the person appearing to be 'doing' or articulating the experience—is actually like an accessory in that it is itself produced by the system and structure of representability. A pre-established network of representational pathways of possibility creates the 'I' of the individual subject in a way that is meaningful. These pathways are established by what followers of Jacques Lacan call the 'Other' (with an uppercase 'O'). We all live—perhaps necessarily—under the Cartesian illusion that 'I' am the authority that decides my next thought, *as if* 'I' now decide I will take a break from writing this passage. Freud broke the Cartesian illusion, which enchanted the Euro-American world since the so-called European Renaissance. In short, my subjective 'I' may bounce along innumerable chains or pathways of representations that furnish the flow of consciousness. But these chains are 'Other' in that 'I' am not the author of these representational possibilities (even though to me, in my Cartesian arrogance, it may feel that I am such an authority). Rather, the system creates the subject. The (compulsively) repetitious condition of representationality creates this subject along pathways and possibilities of meaningfulness that are already established. Since Freud's discoveries, the writings of Friedrich Nietzsche, and the advent of structural linguistics with the lectures of Ferdinand de Saussure, philosophy in the 20th century has established how the pathways and possibilities of representation are established and laid out *for* the subject, not *by* it.

Second: The specific subset of representations that I refer to as pertaining to 'me'—which is also, perhaps confusingly, called the 'subject' *qua* person from an external standpoint—originates performatively from representations expressed by others. My subset of self-representations (those that I take as 'me') is derived, directly or indirectly, from meanings attributed to me by others. The 'me' became constructed in language because people (and things) acted towards me or overtly said to me 'Barnaby is this, Barnaby is that.' This is what Lacanians call the 'other' (with a lowercase 'o'). By repetition, internalization, and modification of their expressions (in the terminology of Jean Piaget, assimilation and accommodation, which are the dual mechanisms of what he calls 'adaptation'), I came to represent 'me' and to develop a 'self-system' derived from the expressed ways in which others represented me. That is, to label myself and know myself as an entity called Barnaby (this derivative character of the 'self' is why toddlers initially refer to themselves in the third-person and only later come to utilize the first-person singular). In short, my psychology was constituted terminologically by the psychology of others. In psychoanalytic jargon, it would be said that the 'self' is formed from the bricolage of its 'object-relational' experiences—with other people, with things, with actions and activities.

In sum, representations of our lived-experience are constituted from outside, from otherness ('Other' and 'other'). On two dimensions—the accessorial character of the 'I' in relation to representationality as a structuring system, and the derivative character of 'me' representations in relation to those articulated by others—otherness is primary. Consequently, the question of what it means to speak one's truth, to come into one's own, or to give an account of oneself has, in many different ways, exercised the most illustrious philosophers of the 20th century. The list would include Laplanche and, quite variously, Theodor Adorno, Emmanuel Levinas, Georges Bataille, Jacques Derrida, Michel Foucault, Luce Irigaray, Julia Kristeva, Gilles Deleuze, Georgio Agamben, Judith Butler, and many others.

Third: But what about amplitudes of lived-experience—dimensions of the psyche—that are unrepresentable yet might have an impact or influence on our inner theatre of representations, even without ever belonging to their construction? Indicated previously, this touches on the possibility that we need to define the psyche as wider and wilder than the summation of those thoughts, feelings, wishes, and fantasies that can be represented. What about forces that might have meaningful consequences for the psyche yet come from 'outside' both the 'I' of representation and the structuring system of representability (forces that are not just other but *otherwise*). I am *not* referring to the so-called 'mind-body problem' and how we consider the way in which the immateriality of psychological functions depends empirically on the materiality of biological operations (as pertinently discussed in my contribution to Jon Mills' 2022 anthology, *Psychoanalysis and the Mind-Body Problem*). Of course, all healers should be interested in how anatomical structures and physiological operations affect our mental operations, but that is not what is to be considered here. Rather, I am suggesting that there might be unrepresented and unrepresentable modes of meaningfulness inherent to our condition. The experiential expression of such modes invites us to listen to them, despite that we cannot capture them in representation. My question here concerns the way in which there might be fields and flows of subtle forces that impact our lived-experience, influencing our inner theatre of thoughts, feelings, wishes, and fantasies, but that nevertheless are themselves not representable—now or in the future. That is, forces that affect the being-becoming of our psyche (ontologically) yet can never be fully understood in terms of any representation of their meaningfulness (epistemologically). In the course of this essay—particularly in Chapter Four, where the question of psychic energy will be addressed—we will find that this question is key to our appreciation of the free-associative method.

So, to set the stage for the remainder of this essay, let us return to the issues of healing and expressiveness. Authentic healing must surely embrace the expression of all aspects and dimensions of that which is to be healed. Its processes will be different for each individual (and there is no ideal state of 'having been healed'). If all aspects and dimensions are not embraced—as indeed they are not in psychotherapy—there may be an extent to which 'healing' will appear benign in some respects but actually will also perpetuate the unnecessary suffering of our lived-experience in other respects. The implication of this is that we might need a method of healing the psyche that goes beyond the limited appreciation of our psyche as a system of representations—beyond psychotherapy. That is, a method that goes beyond the healing that can be achieved by transformation of the representations composing our inner theatre of thoughts, feelings, wishes, and fantasies.

We now know that our self-conscious mind's efforts to heal are inherently problematic, precisely because our reflective self-consciousness is continually engaged in efforts to ward-off other representations that are not to its liking (to put the matter simplistically). Such defensive operations are not self-evident (by which I mean our reflective self-consciousness usually does not know it has engaged them). Psychotherapeutic procedures from Freud to Wittgenstein may be defined as operations that address the mechanisms of defence, bringing representations that were functional but suppressed (and thus descriptively unconscious) into the purview of our self-consciousness. The psyche cannot be healed without labours of representational transformation that are psychotherapeutic (I will later distinguish representational transformation from processes that involve the transmutation of psychic energies).

But—and this is the crucial point—if we are open to the idea that there might be more to our psyche than can ever be properly articulated within the inner theatre of representations, then a method of healing that goes beyond the psychotherapeutic labours of representational transformation is required. That is, a method that would not only enlarge the purview of reflective self-consciousness by listening to representations that have been suppressed and understanding their significance but also by listening to unrepresentable forces that might operate within and upon our psyche—and to become aware of the meaningfulness of their impact *without* attempting to master them representationally. This would be a method that evokes and facilitates a mode of non-representational consciousness, which we will call *awareness* (this is quite distinct from our consciousness, which can be representationally reflected as what is usually called our *self-consciousness*). Such a method takes healing beyond the procedures of psychotherapy, instigating a process of *transmutation* in which ontological or *ontoethical* changes in one's being-becoming take priority over epistemological changes in one's knowing through *transformation* of our representational system. These crucial distinctions of representational transformation (involving self-consciousness, the 'I-Now-Is') versus the transmutative movements of psychic energy, of which there can be an awareness that is unrepresentable (not subjugated to the law and order of narration) will be elaborated as this essay proceeds. It will be demonstrated how free-associative discourse engages such an ontological or ontoethical process of being-becoming over and above anything that can be known epistemologically and psychotherapeutically. The praxis thus secures the unique conditions of psychoanalytic healing.

Note

1 Throughout this essay, I am going to place the term 'psychoanalysis' in scare quotes whenever it refers to healing theories and practices that do *not* prioritize the method of free-association (i.e., almost all the various schools and models that claim to be 'psychoanalytic'). Scare marks are often used when writers wish to distance themselves from a usage that they consider inappropriate. When the term psychoanalysis appears without scare quotes, it refers to what I consider the authentic discipline.

Chapter 2

Introducing free-association

Given that it was the means by which psychoanalysis began as a discipline, it is strikingly paradoxical that the notion of free-associative discourse has never been particularly well investigated or comprehended. Freud discovered this method in the closing years of the 19th century while trying to grasp the meaning of hysterical and other psychiatric symptoms. Yet well over a hundred years after his revolutionary labours—the period in which 'psychoanalysis' has history as a distinctive discipline—there has been a paucity of attempts to understand free-associative processes in their detail and complexity. That is, what free-association is or is not, what different styles of it there may be, why it has the effects that it has, and how it can have such a powerful impact upon processes of personal growth when undertaken in a genuinely psychoanalytic context. In professional publications, psychoanalysts and others often reference the method as significant, as if we all know what it is and what its variations or parameters are. Not enough effort has been directed to all the questions about what it is and why it is important (although there have been some eminent exceptions to this condemnatory generalization, as I shall discuss later).

As previously indicated, this essay is an effort to address and redress such issues. There are serious questions about this method which go unanswered (and often unasked) in the professional literature available in English. These gaps are scarcely remedied by what I have found available in French, German, or Spanish (although I may well have missed some significant items in these

DOI: 10.4324/9781003558262-2

languages). In this context, I propose not only to discuss the topic in a general manner but will necessarily be introducing my own arguments and perspectives. My central thesis is that free-association is necessary to psycho-*analysis* precisely because it is less an epistemological tool (the manner in which it is customarily understood) and more *an ontological or ontoethical way of remobilizing the being-becoming of the subject who free-associates, liberating it from repetition-compulsivity*. That is, not just a method of coming to know something about oneself but far more significantly—in a manner that is quite complex to comprehend—a praxis that frees the subject from imprisonment in its idiopathic patterns of compulsive-repetitiousness.

Psychoanalysis as neither psychotherapy nor counselling

Let us begin with a thought-experiment: Imagine you are chatting with your mythical Great Aunt (or any wise mentor). For the purposes of this experiment, you are telling her about your current woes. You find yourself pouring your heart out, narrating the course of an 18-month affair and how your lover recently dropped you. The rejection was unexpected, seemingly capricious, and excruciatingly painful. You tell the long and emotionally vivid story of this affair, and you give voice to tender thoughts and feelings about the painful break-up. Your Great Aunt knows you well, and she listens concernedly. After a while she says:

> I am so sorry you have been hurt yet again. Clearly this person does not deserve someone as wonderful as you. But have you considered that, ever since you started dating as a young adult, you seem again and again to become passionately attached only to individuals who vacillate quite wildly in their interest in you or in their commitment to you?

If our intent is to understand what psychoanalysis is and is not, we should now ask: Is your Great Aunt actually doing some sort of amateur 'psychoanalysis'? Now imagine this fictitious Great Aunt later adds (caringly, but perhaps rather intrusively):

> You probably don't remember the time in your toddlerhood when your Mother had to go abroad on business for a couple of weeks every month. Do you think you might now be drawn to individuals who dither in their love for you, as if you hope to finally make them settle down with you?

Again, in terms both of her relationship with you and of the speech-acts she offers you (whether or not her assessment of your motives is accurate), let us ask: What is this seemingly wise Great Aunt doing? And finally imagine how this mythical Elder might then get even more immediately personal with you:

> My dear, I know you like our chats, but on the infrequent occasions that you call on me, I find it a bit strange how you act as if you are surprised that I want to see you, but I always do.

This speech-act, now directly addressing how you relate to her—at least from her point of view—again prompts us to ask: Is it some sort of 'psychoanalysis' that your Great Aunt is doing?

The short answer is that Freud, as the founder of psycho-*analysis,* would probably commend your wise Elder's sophistication as a *therapist*. However, I do not believe he would have allowed your conversation with her to be called psychoanalysis, especially if he stuck to the precepts by which he himself defined his discipline. The dialogue cannot be, and can never become, psycho-*analytic* precisely because it avoids any effort towards free-association. In what follows, I am going to develop this argument—on Freud's behalf and for the sake of the future of his discipline.

So what is your Great Aunt doing? Are these imaginary exchanges with her not instances of some sort of 'psycho-analytic'—or proto-psychoanalytic—dialogue? Is this fictively beloved Elder not on the road to becoming an adroit psycho-analyst operating without the—perhaps dubious—benefit of formal training or professional qualification? To answer these questions, let us start by considering what she is indeed accomplishing, so that we can eventually illuminate the significance of what she is not.

Your Great Aunt seems to be a warm and caring individual, clearly concerned for your emotional well-being. She is notably *present* (physically, affectively, cognitively) as she listens caringly to your tales of woe. She is expressly—and we assume genuinely—sympathetic to your heartbreak. She explicitly endorses your self-esteem. She garners various angles of information. She listens to the manifest content of your story (the meanings that you intend her to hear). She also seems to infer some of the possible latent themes of your discourse (the meanings that may or may not have entered your reflective self-consciousness). We can readily imagine that she also attends to your body language, as well as to her own inner reactions evoked by your narrative, both somatic and emotional. She is *empathetic*. Using all this information, she makes inferences on the basis of an implicit theory—or theories—that she has about how humans function in close relationships. I call it an 'implicit theory' (which is a term routinely used by social psychologists) because it seems unlikely that she has ever explicated it in some formalized fashion. Being emotionally present with you, she now applies this theory to produce three different interventions that we assume she hopes will be for your benefit. That is, she intervenes interpretively, very much in the manner that characterizes the labours of a psycho-*therapist*.

First, she invites you to contemplate whether your current sorrow should be understood as the most recent iteration in a series of similar events in your life (it seems that your Great Aunt has some intuition as to the power of the repetition-compulsion over human conduct). By calling your attention to this repetitiousness, she compels you to consider the possibility that you are compulsively drawn to individuals who are destined to thwart your conscious wish for a reliably ongoing partnership.

Second, she goes further when she offers you the idea that your experiences as a toddler with a here-and-then-gone Mother might eventuate into an adult compulsion to master such a trauma by repeatedly trying—of course, without success—to convert flighty friendships, transient flings, or casual hookups into steady partnerships. She tactfully avoids suggesting the possibility that you are drawn to the pain of heartbreak, but we will skip over this additional hypothesis as to your putative emotional masochism.

Third, she then goes even further in applying her theory by drawing your attention to the way you relate to her in the here-and-now. That is, the way you treat her as if her affections for you are fickle when (at least from her point of view) they are not. Couched in the relational here-and-now, this is an interpretation of what has been called—since Freud's earliest papers on psychoanalytic method—a 'transference effect.'

As an aside, note that the question whether this fictitious scenario involves a psychoanalytic process (as contrasted with a psychotherapeutic procedure) is entirely independent of three factors.

First, it does not depend on the qualifications of the practitioner. Your Great Aunt's wisdom did not require formal training nor the display of a fanciful diploma.

Second, it also does not depend on the effectiveness of her commentary; that is, your response to her ideas. Her interventions might well have therapeutic benefit. They might resonate with you and be assimilated by you as pragmatically useful insights. You might come away from this conversation feeling better, feeling soothed by your Great Aunt's evident concern for you, maybe understanding your own relational patterns a little more clearly, perhaps feeling resolved in your determination to guard your heart in future against volatile or indecisive partners. Then again, you might not experience any such therapeutic value. Many conversational procedures have therapeutic benefits, but this does not warrant their being called psychoanalytic (even when their topic is inner thoughts, feelings, wishes, and fantasies).

Perhaps most pertinently, the question whether a 'talking cure' is psychoanalytic cannot depend on whether something that was not-conscious becomes consciously articulated in the course of the conversation. This third point is more contentious. But I will insist on it, not only because there are many meanings of the term 'unconscious' (as will be discussed in Chapter Four) but also because for ideas to come into our reflective self-consciousness is an unremarkable 'event' that occurs moment-to-moment, all-day, every waking day (as well as in moments of our sleeping life). As previously indicated, the term 'reflective self-consciousness' denotes ideas or feelings that one knows one is experiencing because they are represented in what is commonly called our consciousness: 'I know it is 'I' now reading this paragraph.' The gist of your Great Aunt's interpretations of your plight may or may not have been known to you prior to her articulation of them. The themes—that you tend to pursue partners whose availability is unreliable, that you might be trying to resolve the traumas of your toddlerhood, or that these dynamics link with your uncertainty about her affection for you in the here-and-now—may all point to issues that, for want of a better phrasing, have 'never crossed your mind.' Then again, they may be insights hinting at matters that you had dimly considered at some previous juncture but then discarded. They might also be eventualities that are fully familiar to you. After all, familiarity with one's repetition-compulsions does not necessarily disengage or deflate them (as every person who has experienced the limitations of psychotherapy knows well). None of these possibilities constitute criteria as to whether this conversation is psychoanalytic. It is not relevant whether your Great Aunt's speculations are, in some sense, 'correct' assessments of your psychodynamics, especially since psychoanalysis tends to blur the distinction between correct and incorrect (instead finding truthfulness in untruths, and threads of deception even in what purports to be the most refulgent 'truth'). In sum, without substantial explication and qualification, it is not helpful to use 'bringing the unconscious into consciousness' as the critical test as to whether or not a conversation is psychoanalytic.

Psychoanalysis distinguishes itself fundamentally from even the most benign form of counselling, and it goes radically beyond even the most well-conducted versions of psychotherapeutic procedure (or of counselling protocols). There is some overlap because, for psycho-*analysis* to occur, the practitioner must indeed be present and empathetic (as well as warmly caring). Moreover, as I will later discuss, every psychoanalytic treatment begins with a period that is psychotherapeutic. However, this overlap may be deceptive because—as will be elaborated in later chapters—the character and conditions of these qualities in psychoanalysis are differentially special. The fundamental reason why it must be concluded that your Great Aunt is not doing psychoanalysis is that you and she do not immerse yourselves in free-associative processes, prioritizing the power of their movement. She and you are in a discursive procedure, a conversation, that prioritizes *knowing about* your inner theatre of representations. Even if it is the case that in the course of actual treatments psychoanalytic processes are almost invariable preceded by preliminary or preparatory psychotherapeutic procedures, free-association is the prerequisite and priority of any genuinely psychoanalytic discourse (as will be argued in all that follows). An additional and inherently related reason that your Elder's discourse is not psychoanalysis is that it is notably theory-driven. As will be expounded in this essay, psycho-*analysis* is to be defined by its essential commitment to free-associative processes and, in a signature sense, the truthfulness of its discourse is atheoretical (again, it is not an epistemologically-driven trade in interpretations as is psychotherapy).

A psychotherapeutic treatment is always theory-driven, implicitly or explicitly (theoretical precepts govern the epistemological procedures of 'knowing about'). However, the term therapy has become so diluted that nowadays it can refer to any procedure that makes us 'feel better' such that, for many of us, listening to music, pottering in the garden, chatting with a pastoral counsellor, or taking a long hike in beautiful countryside all have therapeutic value. Going beyond merely feeling better, if therapy means acquiring a 'framework of understanding' (a modification in one's system of interpreting oneself and one's world), then an evangelical sermon, a tarot reading that feels spot-on, or an immersion in any number of psychological theories all have therapeutic value (even if this value is markedly different from that promoted by a psychoanalytically-informed or psychoanalytically-oriented psychotherapy). However, if psychotherapy specifically means 'working-through' a conflictual issue in the context of a serious relationship, then your beloved Great Aunt's invitation for you to address with her—in a context of complete candour and confidentiality—whatever ambivalence you are performing in your relationship with her definitely opens up the possibility of a relationship that has therapeutic value. But this does not make her efforts proto-psychoanalytic, despite how much of a blessing her endeavours may be to you.

Regrettably, Freud often used the terms psychoanalysis and psychotherapy as if they were interchangeable. Yet more unfortunately, his focus on the method that distinguishes psychoanalysis got lost around 1914, after which he became heavily preoccupied with the construction of his grand and influential theories of mental functioning (ego, id, superego or ego-ideal, object-relations, narcissism, splitting, and so forth). Indeed, he seems at times to have identified his discipline with these theories, although in his clearer mind he definitely did not. Until the end of his life, he knew that the discipline should not be identified with his theorizing, his 'witch metapsychology' (which is how he named it in his 1937 essay *Analysis Terminable and Interminable*). Rather, psychoanalysis is fundamentally and foremost a method. That is, the method of free-associative processes. Moreover, this is not method-*qua*-technique but rather method-*qua*-praxis (as will be shortly discussed). So let us now turn to the history by which the appreciation of free-association somehow became occluded, both in Freud's lifetime and in the subsequent history of his discipline.

Freud's loss of focus on method

Although he became so preoccupied with formulating the life of the mind theoretically, there is clear evidence that Freud was always of the opinion that a conversational procedure—or any other mode of discourse—is not going to become psycho-*analytic* unless free-associative processes are centrally prioritized. The public's general understanding today (supported by undergraduate textbooks) is that 'psychoanalysis' is a set of theoretical frameworks (such as ego-psychology or object-relations) that are, or were, yoked to a procedure of psychotherapeutic treatment, which many texts now caricature as being outdated. How did this come about? In the contemporary context, it is legitimate, indeed vital, that we ask what this discipline is (or was) and whether the definition or delineation of it has changed at all usefully over the 13 decades of its history?

We are accustomed to assuming that the history of human affairs is—almost relentlessly—progressive. Steadily (or not quite so steadily), our species makes advances. From our hominid ancestry to the 21st century, we make improvements, become more accomplished, and comprehend the world ever more skillfully. Clearly, progress does indeed characterize the history of technology, from crude stone weapons to nuclear warheads.

However, whether the history of our species is progressive in terms of moral and political affairs is far more open to debate. Recently, some very scholarly historians and philosophers have argued impressively that there is scant evidence that humans treat each other, or understand each other, any better today than they did centuries or even millennia ago. Sometimes wisdom—and profound insight—does not develop progressively but gets lost within the profusion of mistaken developments that present themselves as progress. In now charting the history of 'psychoanalytic' thinking about free-association, we will come to realize that appreciation for this unique mode of expression has generally diminished—and almost been lost—with what are, I believe, disastrous consequences for the discipline.

Freud discovered, or initiated, the discipline of psychoanalysis in two decades of clinical working and playing both within his patients' and within his own inner world (let us adopt the notion of 'workplaying' in this essay because it nicely conveys the spirit of free-association). That was between approximately 1895 and 1914. Early in this period he experimented with a number of techniques and procedures by which to investigate the occurrences of his own mind and those of his patients (e.g., the use of cocaine, hypnosis, authoritarian suggestion, interrogatory trickery, speculation about the meaning of slips and jokes, as well as, perhaps most significantly, the systematic deconstruction of dreams). But he quite rapidly concluded that listening to the trajectories of free-association is not just the optimal, but the exclusively viable, method for opening us to the dynamics of the—repressed—unconscious, as he came to understand it.

Concurrently, he broke away from the psychotherapeutic technique of 'controlled' or 'experimental association' pioneered by Jung. With the latter, the research subject is offered a word-stimulus such as 'hedgehog' and responds 'prickly' or with some other reaction. In a sense, Freud only retained this controlled procedure when he would ask patients to associate to a specific element of a dream that the patient had reported free-associatively (we will later address this exception, which is key to the all-important contribution he made in his 1900 *Traumdeutung*). In significant disagreement with Jung, Freud generally insists on the patient's spontaneity and his method is thus 'free' in a specific sense (that will be illuminated in later chapters). It has rightly been argued (by commentators such as Axel Hofer) that Freud should have adhered to his alternate term *freier Einfalle*, rather than *freie Assoziation*, because the former strongly implies the receptivity or 'passivity' of surrendering any sense of control so as to allow the next idea to 'fall into' consciousness. The notion of *freier Einfalle* entails the opening of consciousness becoming receptive to material entering its purview as if from outside—material that can enter our awareness without being able to be nailed down by our representational self-consciousness. The term abolishes the connotation of intentionality that inevitably accompanies Jung's 'experimental' or 'controlled' association.

Shortly, we will discuss why free-association is a method or praxis, and not a technique. But here we should note in passing that Freud was never entirely closed-minded about other ways of working psycho-*therapeutically*. Indeed, in a 1910 paper on a 'wild' procedure, he commented not unfavourably on the actions of a physician who told his patient to masturbate or get married in order to overcome her neurosis (a physician, we might note, who is substantially wilder than your kindly and tactful Great Aunt). Freud is quite open to techniques other than free-association as potentially successful procedures of psycho-*therapy* (or even counselling), but clearly that does not imply that they could replace the unique processes of psycho-*analysis*.

In this period from 1895 to around 1914, Freud arrives at, and consolidates, his commitment to the method or praxis of free-associative speaking and listening. That is, method as contrasted with technique. Techniques involve a technology of application in relation to an explicit or explicatable theoretical framework (your Great Aunt's theory may be implicit, but it is in principle explicatable). With technique, there is a set of ideas as to how things should function—a theory—then there is a procedure of application that uses these preconceptions manipulatively to transform how things are actually operating. Psychotherapy of any variety involves techniques that are derived from theory, and it is invariably performed within a manipulative (and authoritarian) relationship. By contrast, psychoanalytic processes, as the singular exemplar of free-associative method, are inherently anti-technical (anti-theoretical and anti-authoritarian).

Opposed to technique, the notion of *praxis* implies an exploratory or revelatory method both that is not governed by an explicit or implicit framework of preconceptions and that changes the 'thing' or 'object'—by allowing it to change itself—as the optimal way to become aware of its functioning. Thus, changing the object's being-becoming is the prime mode of praxis, and knowing about the object is at most derivative. The constitutive mutuality of 'subject' and 'object' is thus radically different from that inscribed in any conventional epistemology. 'Helpful Ideas'—auxiliary to the change process—may arise along the way, but these are treated as provisional notions, to be deployed, interrogated, and ultimately discarded. Thus, any formulation of 'what's what' is at most a temporary byproduct of the change process and is not the endpoint of the intervention. Freud called these auxiliary ideas his *Hilfvorstellungen* (badly translated in James Strachey's Standard Edition as 'conceptual scaffolding'). Their provisional status highlights the dynamic character and conditions of praxis, in which 'understanding'—in any sense of the term—is at most a consequence of change, not the cause of it and not the prime goal of the venture. We will shortly return to the notion of free-association as praxis because it is crucial to any appreciation of the way in which psychoanalysis is authentically psycho-*analytic*.

Arguably, in the twenty years during which the method of psychoanalysis was birthed, Freud deployed relatively few *Hilfvorstellungen*. He had the notion that ideas (representations of thoughts and feelings) could be variously invested, disinvested, or divested with psychic energy, which would result in their variable intensity in relation to reflective consciousness. He also had the notion that ideas could lose their energetic investment such that they became *repressed* or 'lost in translation'—yet remaining clandestinely but actively impactful on the representational domain of self-consciousness. But not much else mattered for the initiation of psychoanalysis, *except* his finding that the most forbidden ideas, those that violated the incest taboo, operated *as if* they had crossed a 'barrier' (this then being considered the hallmark of repression, as will be discussed). Effectively that is all Freud had for him to become convinced of the unique properties of free-associative praxis and of their necessity for psychoanalysis.

So, how did 20 years of experimentation with a method get displaced by Freud's subsequently accelerating preoccupation with constructing grand theories of the mind? In the pre-1914 period of discovery, the definition of his discipline was notably specific and strikingly radical. It was not to be a psychology that was dependent upon the ordinary elaborations of consciousness, nor was it to be a science that begins by examining (or caring too much about) the neuronal functioning of the brain. Rather, psychoanalysis was to be appreciated as a journey of an adventure with radically experiential, experimental, and existential implications. That is, the depth exploration of a person's thoughts, feelings, actions, and fantasies, by means of this specific method—free-association and only free-association. Even a cursory reading of Freud's 1900 masterwork on the meaning of dreams makes this evident (*Traumdeutung* would perhaps have been better translated as the *Meaning of Dreams*, rather than the customary *Interpretation of Dreams*). Psychoanalysis explores meanings and—more precisely—it explores meanings that appear to be hidden by other meanings or precluded by the otherwise condition of their meaningfulness.

In over 40 years of writing about psychoanalysis (from 1895, almost until his death in 1939), Freud was so creatively prolific that the intellectual and scientific trajectory of his thinking is open to being read in several ways. His thinking was far from monolithic. As I have already indicated, it is an error to imagine that Freud's intellectual and clinical journey was entirely progressive (one moment of understanding leading inexorably to yet deeper and more powerful comprehensions). This is because, as I shall suggest, he occasionally seems to lose focus on some of his own most important insights. Moreover, although the tone of his writings is typically magisterial, he often exemplifies the honesty of equivocation, and he is sometimes self-contradictory, especially when he reflects on the—epistemological and ontological or ontoethical—character of the discipline he founded.

To give just a single telling example: In 1913, while struggling to explain psychoanalysis to psychologists and philosophers, he predicts in passing that conflict with what he called *offiziellen Wissenshaft* ('official science') is likely to be the destiny of his discipline. Yet in an encyclopaedia article a decade later, he insists that his discipline takes its place as 'the scientific pursuit of the psychical unconscious.' Whereas in 1933 he suggests in neo-Kantian fashion that there are two separate sciences, psychology and natural science, about five years later he writes that his discipline is 'a natural science like any other.'

In order to set the stage for the rest of this essay on the praxis of free-association, I am offering a specific way of reading Freud's trajectory. This reading is—I would argue strenuously—no more tendentious than any other.

Around 1914, one can detect a slight but significant cesura or turning-point in the style and content of his writings. Other Freud scholars have noted this, such as André Green in 1974. Indeed—I am proposing—there is a critical sense in which, after just two decades of free-associative practice, the definition of what is and is not psychoanalysis begins to go haywire. The discipline increasingly becomes designated and delimited not in terms of praxis (that is, the engagement with a unique method of change). Rather it comes to refer to a set of theories about mental functioning that are then instrumentally applied (objectivistically or inter-subjectivistically) as techniques for the psychotherapeutic manipulation of the patient.

As an aside, a sketch of his post-1914 theory-building might adhere to the following outline. In 1914, Freud launched a theory of narcissism that would become—in a rather tortuous way—one of the bases for post-Freudian theories of the self. In 1915, he elaborated a spatialized depiction of the mind, a topography that made it seem as if our representations (thoughts, feelings, wishes, and fantasies) are shunted between locations (conscious, preconscious, unconscious) by energetic forces (*Triebe*, 'drives'). In 1918, his essay on mourning and melancholia laid the groundwork for what would later be developed in sophisticated theories of object-relations. Then in 1920, he wrote a speculative monograph on the role of lifefulness and deathfulness in psychic life (this is the specific way that Laplanche and I, as well as others, read this important but challenging text). Three years later, Freud presented the structural-functional framework (ego, id, superego, and ego-ideal) that, after another three years, was to be supported in 1926 by an influential theory of signal anxiety. The latter would prepare his most ardent followers, in the 1930s and thereafter, to launch more complex theories of the ego organization and its mechanisms of defence. Just before his death, building on his 1927 discussion of fetishism, Freud wrote a seminal paper on the 'splitting' of the ego organization, which was not published until 1940. This would provide a conceptual platform for the later advent of psychotherapies promulgated by the followers of Melanie Klein with their stellar concept of projective identification. The seemingly small but crucial question I am raising—in offering this synopsis of Freud's impressive record of ambitious efforts to theorize our mental functioning—is as follows: With all these magnificent efforts of theory-building, did psycho-*analysis* with the defining priority of its original method actually get lost?

Freud must have sensed the tension between an experiential commitment to the free-associative method and the objectivistic construction of theoretical models of the human mind. Theories of intrapsychic or interpersonal functioning may be constructed on the basis of sources other than experience with free-associative praxis, and they may generate techniques of psychotherapeutic transformation that do not require free-association. In a certain sense, Freud was caught in a bind that he himself almost certainly did not understand sufficiently. We may think of it as follows.

In the conception of science that has dominated modern eurocentric culture for the past 300 to 500 years—known to philosophers in terms of the analytico-referential or logical-empiricist masterdiscourse—a 'method' or technique generates findings or data that can then be organized as a theoretical construction, and theories govern techniques that can be used instrumentally to effect change. This is a somewhat oversimplified depiction because theoretical propositions—notably 'hypotheses'—influence the methods of 'discovery' that are used, as well as the ways in which they are used. As was indicated in the previous chapter, here it is important to note that, contrary to the hegemonic myths surrounding the philosophies of analytico-referentiality or logical-empiricism, an *ontological* commitment as to what sort of *being-becoming* is to be investigated necessarily precedes any *epistemological* decision on how to advance our *knowing* about it by making it an object of investigation (including when the 'object' is itself an other's mind or reflectively the subject's own mind). To give a mundane example of the popular notion of this term, the method or technique of looking down a microscope offers us new perceptual experiences—'findings'—that can then be codified or 'made sense of' within the theoretical frameworks of various sciences. This is an epistemological activity that we commonly and rather crudely call 'science.' Note that, before you invent, build and use a microscope, there is a fundamental sense in which you have already determined what sort of entity is going to be scrutinized (samples of sections of tissue that might be pathological, unicellular organisms that might contaminate your water supply, or even, with a transmission compound microscope, molecular structures). Freud may well have believed—somewhat confusedly—that what he was doing comprised this sort of science; as if free-association were equivalent to the technique of microscopy. Indeed, occasionally he explicitly compared his practices to the act of looking through a microscope (or telescope). Sometimes, especially after 1914, he may well have considered free-associative 'findings' to be data from which he would construct his grand theories. Indeed, these theories do have some sort of derivation from Freud's experimentation with free-associative process, or at least he was convinced they did. But their formulation clearly also draws on many other, very different, facets of Freud's highly erudite capacity to observe and make sense of the lived-experiences of our species (from his devotion to jokes to his erudite readings of literature, archaeology, mythology, and so forth). In short, these grand theories might have been formulated without the experiential labours of free-association. Indeed many of Freud's theoretical ideas have been traced back to classical and medieval philosophies (as well as to the germanophone influences of 19th-century writers such as Arthur Schopenhauer, Johan Wolfgang Goethe, and Friedrich Schelling).

There is evidence that Freud also knew—or sort of knew—that the prime importance of the free-associative method might not be as a step in an epistemological procedure. Perhaps he knew that only derivatively can it be regarded epistemologically as a 'method' or technique for gathering data. Rather, it is primarily the *praxis of healing*, an ontological 'method' (or better, a method that is ontoethical). That is, free-association is a discourse that facilitates an emergence—or reinvigoration—of the being-becoming of the individual who diligently engages in this process. This is far more weighty than whatever contributions the method might make as a data-gathering procedure aimed at formulating—within the context of a theoretical framework—the occurrences of the person's inner world.

It seems that Freud was somewhat aware of this overlooked incongruity within his thinking because even in the years in which he was immersed in the formulation of his objectivistic theories he continued to insist that free-association is the *sine qua non* of his discipline (one finds such pronouncements in his lectures and writings of 1916–1917, 1924, 1925, and 1937). Arguably, free-associative process *is* psychoanalysis, and whatever is done without free-association is not. Contrary to the aphorism attributed Sándor Ferenczi that 'the patient is not cured by free-association,' Freud had some sense that engagement with the method is, in and of itself, curative—regardless of the interpretations that may be formulated *post hoc* about the contents that surface in the course of free-associative processes.

It may or may not be overstated to conclude that Freud was confused about the epistemological and ontological (ontoethical) status of the very 'method' that he claimed was essential to the processes of psycho-*analysis*. He would have been somewhat familiar with the controversies sparked by neo-Kantian philosophers of the Marburg and Heidelberg Schools over the distinction between *naturwissenschaft* and *geisteswissenschaft* (natural versus human or 'spirit' sciences). But there was little support for him to pioneer the distinction between the epistemology of 'method' as a (natural) scientific technique in the usual sense *versus* the ontological or ontoethical and existential implications of 'method' as praxis. As already indicated, any increment of knowing with the latter method is derivative from the processes of changing the being-becoming of—such as they are—both subject and object. As far as I am aware, there is no evidence that Freud knew of this distinction such that he could insist on it—yet this is precisely the type of method that he instigated.

Despite its ancient Greek roots, praxis is best explicated by Hegelian philosophers such as August Cieszkowski in 1838 and Karl Marx in his early manuscripts. It is unlikely that Freud gave much, in any, consideration to the implications of this particular lineage of philosophical writings. Praxis is notably a processive method that changes the character of things, their history, even as it understands them. This entails an entirely different relation between them, as reflected in Karl Marx's aphorism that the point is not to further interpret the world but to change it. Freud would surely have known the aphorism, but there is little or no direct evidence that he was impacted by it. Such a notion, proposing that one only knows a thing by changing it, is surely germane to an appreciation of the power of free-associative discourse.

In addition to these considerations, it must be acknowledged how desperate Freud was to establish himself at the head of a redoubtably scientific movement, and how this may have pressured him—wittingly or unwittingly—not to be too forthright in defining his discipline in terms of its method. Fame as a scientist meant that he had to build theories (with psychotherapeutic techniques of application) so that he could position his discipline as a natural science concordant with the medical model. It might be recalled that it was more or less at the time of Freud's medical training that Carl von Rokitansky founded the 'New Vienna School of Medicine'—breaking with 'natural philosophies' of healing and establishing medicine as an exclusively logical-empiricist science. It can well be argued that as a consequence of his ambition to be esteemed within the circles espousing such ideology Freud would have been defensive about defining his discipline in terms of what we can now appreciate as a mode of praxis directed towards our own psychic functioning.

How psychoanalysis got lost in its theories of mental functioning

Rarely, if ever, can revolutionary vision be secured and advanced by means of organizational establishment or bureaucratic regulation. Nevertheless, in wanting to be at the head of an acclaimed scientific—in the logical-empiricist sense—movement, Freud founded the International Psychoanalytic Association (IPA) in 1910 with the assistance not only of Jung and Ferenczi but also of major figures such as Ernest Jones, Karl Abraham, and Otto Rank. The mandate was to perpetuate and propagate the discipline initiated by Freud. As of 2025, this organization boasts a membership of over 12,000 individuals who claim to be 'psychoanalysts.' However, it is quite telling that less than two years after the IPA's establishment Freud felt it necessary to establish a 'Secret Committee' composed of Jones, Abraham, Ferenczi, and Rank, along with Hans Sachs (Max Eitingon and Anna Freud were recruited later). The purpose of this clandestine group was supposedly to protect Freud's discipline from doctrinal deviations. However, given its secrecy, we have little or no way of knowing the Committee's deliberations, let alone how they defined the specifics of their self-appointed task. Plans for expulsions from the IPA may well have been discussed, but it seems quite likely that the Committee was less of a covert vanguard or functioning commissariat and more of a cheerleading squad for its esteemed leader.

Let us digress slightly to consider the role that the IPA has played in the progress, or regress, of psychoanalytic thinking, because it is an ignominious trajectory in which the priority of the distinguishing method became almost entirely forgotten—and thus the definition and delineation of the discipline has more or less descended into incoherence. To this day, it seems highly ambiguous how the IPA claims to perpetuate, propagate, and guard over a discipline it finds overly challenging to define.[1]

It is far from outlandish to suggest that today over 90% of the certified members of the IPA would be unable, or at least hard-pressed, to explain how or why the fictitious conversation with your Great Aunt is not an inchoate instance of amateur psychoanalysis. Several studies, such as that reported in Kate Schechter's *Illusions of a Future*, offer evidence for this assertion. Interview your local 'psychoanalysts' and you will find that certified practitioners routinely revert to distinctions that are procedural rather than processive. Notably, your wise Elder has not asked you to lie on a couch; you are not seeing her several times each week; she lacks certain sorts of professionalism (she does not charge you a fee, not keeping the conversation to a fixed limit of

45 or 50 minutes, and *plaise à dieu* she hugs and kisses you at the beginning and at the end of each meeting).

In terms of demarcating the discipline for which it purports to advocate, the IPA as an organization does little better than its average member. Disciplinary definition often reverts to the historical lodestar 'as founded by Freud' or deploys routinized references to the 'unconscious' and to 'transferences' in the clinical setting. This hardly ameliorates the issue. As will be discussed in Chapter Four, the term 'unconscious' has at least a half-dozen meanings and is rarely utilized with much precision. Scarcely any more helpful are the notions of 'transference' (the feelings you, as patient, have for your Great Aunt and how you act towards her) and 'countertransference' (the feelings and reactions your Great Aunt has towards you, and how she tries to use them to help you see matters about yourself more clearly). According to all these rhetorically bolstered criteria, your Elder might seem to be performing at least somewhat psychoanalytically, but in the absence of any pretence at free-associative discourse, she actually is not (and, as I have suggested, it seems very unlikely that Freud would have credited her with doing so).

It is not that the IPA is—should be, or should have been—hidebound in its definition and delimitation of the discipline it purports to advance. Rather, the problem is that it has, from the start, been an organization more concerned with its own politics (and with guardianship of the guild) than with deepening our understanding of psychoanalytic processes. Over the course of its history, its self-perpetuating politics have become increasingly paradoxical in this regard. Procedurally, there are all sorts of hoops and hazing rituals that a candidate-trainee has to undergo in order to become a full member of an IPA-approved institute or society. Yet ideologically or intellectually (dare one say, *scientifically*), its collective comprehension of the discipline it is supposedly protecting is ultra-liberal or, more precisely, ultra-vague, indeed otiose to the egregious point of laxity.

Many members of the IPA will, when asked, define psychoanalysis in terms of the particular theory to which they subscribe. An ego-psychological psychotherapist will tell you 'psychoanalysis' is the therapeutic technique that examines mental phenomena as compromise formations (between reality, id, and superego or ego-ideal). The ego-oriented psychotherapist interprets them as such so that the patient can generate new compromises that are more adaptive ('adaption' is, since Heinz Hartmann's writings, a concept loaded with bourgeois values). A Kleinian psychotherapist will tell you that the discipline must be understood and defined by techniques that respond to infantile mental phenomena in terms of their potential advance between paranoid-schizoid and depressive positions (containing patients interpretively so that they can mature emotionally towards the latter). Both define the discipline in terms of theory and technique. Yet the common ground between them, despite their 1940 'Discussions' (the resulting armistice can scarcely be said to be authentic), has proved somewhat insubstantial. Both continue to vie for positions of power within the IPA.

The IPA has become the professional—yet somewhat incoherently misshapen—home for practitioners from divergent sects and schools, some with entirely contradictory views of the human condition. This is worth noting, since none of these factions appreciate the fundamental necessity of free-associative praxis. For example, the theories upheld by Kleinian practitioners and those upheld by followers of Heinz Kohut (self-psychologists and many of the subsequent 'relational school') involve assumptions about the character of the newborn infant that are diametrically opposite. One baby is overwhelmed by its own violent impulses of envy towards the maternal breast. The other comes into the world blissfully ready to take up its position centre stage (although it is always vulnerable to disappointments and frustrations due to its caretaker's empathetic inadequacies). Another example: On one side, the heirs of Hartmann, Anna Freud, and David Rapaport (contemporary structural-functional theorists, from Jacob Arlow and Merton Gill to Dale Boesky and Gertrude Blanck) approach the adult's mental organization or 'ego' as unavoidably contending with conflicts involved in its management of three or four quasi-external forces (id impulses, superego, and ego-ideal, as well as reality as the ego constructs it). By contrast, self-psychologists, relational-psychologists, and interpersonal 'psychoanalysts,' from William Alanson White and Kohut to Stephen Mitchell and

Jessica Benjamin, posit a comparatively integrated—or potentially integrated—inner life for the individual, who has to manage dialogically a multitude of 'me-you' connections, and for whom the unconscious is little more than a matter of 'selective inattention' and deeper modes of suppression.

In short, the proverbial alien from a far-away galaxy, whose job is to report back to its superiors concerning the affairs of earthlings, would look at the world's population of 'psychoanalysts' sheltered under the banner of the IPA and find it impossible to demarcate the discipline to which they supposedly adhere. The IPA's forward movement is maintained by dubious strategies of guild membership, if for no other reason than that it is surely impossible to advocate authentically for a 'discipline' that harbours such conflicting sects and schools. And yet, 'psychoanalysis' continues to be upheld, its definition and delineation being articulated in terms of a diversity of techniques and theories.

Free-association in recent decades

As should be evident by now, the reason that so many practitioners would probably fumble over the question whether your mythical Great Aunt is an inchoate psychoanalyst is that most practitioners understand their clinical labours as the technical application of one or other theory of mental functioning. The theories used may differ, but the relationship between theory and technique is held in common, and the clinical process is understood to be primarily epistemological. New ways of knowing (meaning new representational formulations of the inner operations of the mind) are seemingly used, as if instrumentally, to produce changes in the patient's existence or being-becoming. Theory governs the application of technique and thus some sort of understanding is produced, which causes some sort of change that has the structure of a 'new' repetition-compulsion. This is method-as-technique. By contrast, method-as-praxis might change the way the psyche operates by opening awareness to dimensions of meaningfulness that are otherwise than representation—and this is what a diligent commitment to free-association can achieve. Such a commitment prioritizes the (re)mobilization of our being-becoming over the labours of constructing new, but quasi-static, formulations of knowledge—interpretations, insights, and so forth. Understandings may arise provisionally and transiently from this praxis of changeful movement, but the ontoethical processes of change are foremost, as they unlock the subject's discourse from repetition-compulsivity.

The consequence of the all-too-prevalent prioritization of epistemology is that the current disciplinary literature in 'psycho-analysis' only tends to refer—as if in passing—to the importance of free-association. It does no more than that because, in an epistemological framework, other techniques of 'data-gathering' are equally viable for the representational transformations that are intended. This situation, in which free-association is upheld rhetorically (that is, without substantial understanding of its being psycho-*analytically* essential), led Irwin Hoffman in 2006 to declare that the method is 'one of the sacred cows of the psychoanalytic tradition.' His verdict is understandable, although psychoanalytically mistaken. It is mistaken because Hoffman does not grasp the significance of this praxis as a process of listening *not only* to that which is suppressed within the psyche *but also* to that which is the unconscious-as-repressed (and thus neither represented nor potentially representable). It can be noted that his professional allegiance is to relational or 'dialectically constructivist' psychotherapy, in which the 'unconscious' is relegated to that which can be articulated through dialogical procedures of 'me-you' encounter. Yet his verdict is understandable not only because the distinction between a psychotherapeutic procedure and a psychoanalytic process (and thence between the suppressed and repressed unconscious) has been all but completely lost. It is also understandable because, since Freud's earliest writings, there is so little literature examining the what, how, and why of free-association and thus little basis on which to defend the method as the praxis by which representational discourse deconstructs itself and thus opens itself to the otherwise voicing of the unconscious-as-repressed (as will be elaborated in Chapter Four).

An eminent example of the extent to which, and the way in which, any appreciation of the centrality of the free-associative method to a genuinely psycho-*analytic* treatment has been almost entirely lost has been splendidly (but disastrously) presented to us in the writings of David Tuckett. Over several decades, Tuckett convened two or more international (and multilingual) working groups to engage in comparative research on varied treatments conducted by 'psychoanalysts.' With no less than 19 collaborators, his two book-length reports on their deliberations now seem like indispensable reading for anyone trying to fathom the contemporary state of this discipline (in its predominantly Euro-American incarnation): *Psychoanalysis Comparable and Incomparable* was published in 2008, and *Knowing What Psychoanalysts Do and Doing what Psychoanalysts Know* in 2024. There is so much detailed information and insightful opinion that could be explored and evaluated in these volumes that their review is beyond the scope of this essay. I will make only three points.

First, ultimately the discussions place a premium on knowledge as the most significant motor of psychoanalytic change—that is, knowing as the formation of representations that are cogent, coherent, and correspondent with the phenomena that are to be known. In this respect, it is as if the group's labours are a heroic effort to organize the practices of different versions of 'psychoanalysis' within the underlying framework of the analytico-referential or logical-empiricist masterdiscourse.

Second, there is next to no mention of—let alone engagement with—the thinking of the Lacanian and post-Lacanian lineages. Yet, many would judge Lacan's 1958 paper, 'The Direction of the Treatment and the Principles of its Power,' to be one of the 20th century's most important presentations on the character and conditions of psychoanalytic processes (in addition to the early years of his *Séminaires*). Indeed, it initiates his effort to rescue 'psychoanalysis' from its deterioration into what he discerns as its anti-Freudian tendencies (and perhaps for this reason alone, the enterprise gets ignored). Moreover, contemporary Lacanian writing on free-association, such as that of Gabriel Lombardi, which is some of the most usefully provocative—even if problematic, as will be indicated in the next chapter—is ignored. An assortment of francophone contributors, who are, in a sense, post-Lacanian, is also neglected (for example, Jean-Luc Donnet, Green, Kristeva, and Laplanche).

Third, as might be predictable, these two volumes give scant attention, even indirectly, to free-association. It is mentioned very sporadically as a technique (its significance is thereby presumptively demoted). However, even thinking in terms of technique rather than praxis, it is frankly astonishing (or perhaps not, given what I have described in this chapter) how much of the anglophone literature on free-association Tuckett's groups managed to ignore. The standout examples being that Anton Kris' distinguished monograph, *Free Association: Method and Process*, is never cited; Christopher Bollas' eminent writings receive only a passing citation (and that, to one of his minor papers in a German translation); and Marita Torsti-Hagman's monumental work, *Harvesting Free Association*, is entirely ignored. Yet these are landmarks in any discussion of free-association (and I will engage them with critical appreciation in the next chapter). Also seemingly significant omissions are the anglophone contributions of diverse writers such as Jill Gentile, Michael Eigen, Henry Zvi Lothane, Thomas Ogden, Dominique Scarfone, and Guy Thompson.

In sum, the ginormous and glamorous efforts of Tuckett's group, which many 'psychoanalysts' will consider nothing less than heroic, are perhaps as significant for what they leave out as they are for what they consider. They are indicative of an approach which pre-determines that 'psychoanalysis' will only be examined in hegemonic terms of theory and technique. The group's efforts are indeed symptomatic of how far free-association has become demoted and disregarded within the field of 'psychoanalysis' today. So, let us now proceed to its reintroduction.

Note

1 For the purposes of this thesis and without any particular disrespect, I will sidestep the membership of two rival organizations, the International Federation of Psychoanalytic Societies (founded by Erich Fromm in 1962 as a consortium of organizations that position themselves as being doctrinally dissentient from the IPA), and the World Association of Psychoanalysis (launched in 1992 as a Lacanian protest against the hegemony of the IPA, and currently claiming 2,000 members).

Chapter 3

On speaking free-associatively

The conspicuous and ultimately central feature of free-association is that it is far from a conventional way of speaking. It is not normal. It pushes against the bounds of normativity and transgresses the rules and regulations of ordinary conversation. In short, to utter, or to attempt to utter, every thought, feeling, wish or fantasy out loud in the presence of another person is an abnormality that—if engaged fully and in public—would be liable to incite reactions that result in the speaker being socially stigmatized, ostracized, banished, or institutionalized.

This is why the process, undertaken by the patient in the presence of a relatively silent psychoanalyst, has to be contained to ensure what Adam Limentani summarized as its fundamental sense of intimacy, freedom, and safety. That is, properly contained by the patient's own resistances to associating freely, by the psychoanalyst's presence with all its strange significance, and by the so-called 'frame' of the treatment (the punctual and precise beginning and ending of a 50 minute session, the scheduled spacing of no more than a few days between sessions, and the transaction of a professional fee paid by the patient to ensure the psychoanalyst's reasonable standard of living).

There is more to the aporia of free-association than its engagement within a special frame that is socioculturally unconventional. There is a crucial question as to what extent the method's expressive processes contravene the rules and regulations of narration by exceeding the law and order of 'making sense,' which, in my 1993 book, was dubbed the 'narratological imperative.' In the context

DOI: 10.4324/9781003558262-3

of an appreciation of the riskiness or wildness of genuine free-association and the question of its nonconformity to or transgression of the narratological imperative, I will introduce in this chapter a heuristic distinction between 'soft' story-telling and full-on 'radical' processes of free-association. But before moving to this exposition, it will be useful to discuss briefly the way in which patients are launched—or launch themselves—into these processes.

Procedures of embarkation

Although patients are not in psychoanalysis to follow the psychoanalyst's instructions (indeed, compliant attitudes operate against the movement of psychoanalytic processes), how free-association is portrayed at the outset of a treatment is not without impact or influence, even if the 'instruction' usually has to be repeatedly discussed in the initial phase of most treatments.

In the context of Freud's shift from method-as-praxis (pre-1914) to the more theory-governed standpoint of method-as-technique (as discussed in the previous chapter), it is telling how his way of requiring the patient to begin free-associating shifted accordingly. In 1913, Freud recommends the patient be instructed as follows:

> What you tell me must differ in one respect from an ordinary conversation. Ordinarily you rightly try to keep a connecting thread running through your remarks and you exclude any intrusive ideas that may occur to you and any side-issues, so as not to wander too far from the point. But in this case you must proceed differently … Act as though, for instance, you were a traveler sitting next to the window of a railway carriage and describing to someone inside the carriage the changing views which you see outside …

By 1923, the year in which the structural-functional model was announced, the tone of Freud's instruction is modified. He advocates telling the patient to assume:

> … the position of an attentive and dispassionate self-observer, merely to read off all the time the surface of his [*sic*]

> consciousness, and on the one hand to make a duty of the most complete honesty while on the other not to hold back any idea from communication, even if he feels that it is too disagreeable or if he judges that it is nonsensical or too unimportant or irrelevant to what is being looked for …

As I have previously discussed elsewhere, the difference between these two injunctions indicates a conservative revisioning. Missing in 1923 is the original double mandate to forgo trying to 'keep a connecting thread' or being concerned about wandering 'too far from the point.' The 1913 analogy to the passivity of being on a train ride is replaced by the objectivistic and scientistic injunction to be active as an 'attentive and dispassionate self-observer.' This surely characterizes the method as that of data-gathering. The tone of 1913 suggests a submissiveness—surrender—in relation to the stream of consciousness, merely noting and articulating the thoughts, feelings, wishes, and fantasies that *fall into* the patient's purview. It is noteworthy that around these years Freud would occasionally refer to *freie Assoziation* as *freier Einfalle.* As mentioned earlier, the latter suggests a poetic process rather than a technical one. That is, a process in which, instead of holding onto the magisterial illusion that one is in control of one's next idea, one surrenders so as to allow thoughts, feelings, wishes, and fantasies to arise within—or 'fall into'—the ambit of consciousness. Finally, it should be noted that, contrary to this submissive-poetic attitude, the 1923 instruction manifestly indicates that something is 'being looked for,' even if the patient is supposed not to prejudge what it is or where it is to be found. Here again the method has clearly become a technique of data-gathering, rather than an amplification or liberation of the patient's being-becoming.

It should also be noted that both versions pose a gap between the speaking patient and the flow of representations coming into consciousness; as if there is a subject observing an 'object,' albeit its own self or itself-as-object. We might think of this as the gap of translation and reportage. This is an important issue because shortly I will suggest that—with what I call full-on or radical free-association—such a gap diminishes. It lessens as the process facilitates the ontological or ontoethical mobilization of the patient's being-becoming (and radially departs from the epistemological procedure of 'knowing about' whatever is occurring experientially). This is *not* to imply that such a gap is other than beneficial psycho-*therapeutically*. Consider here the usefulness of a patient developing a 'self-observing ego' function, 'psychological mindedness,' and a reflective capacity, or a 'self-analytic attitude' as described by Richard Sterba and others. But beneficial psychotherapeutic procedures are only characteristic of the initial phase of a psychoanalytic treatment (which is generally found to be the first year of a treatment). As will be demonstrated, psychoanalysis has effects beyond those of psychotherapeutically enhancing the patient's repertoire of representations.

There are several other ways of presenting to the patient what Freud considered the basic or fundamental rule of psychoanalytic discipline. He called this the *Grundregel* (sometimes *Hauptregel*), which certainly implies that the rule is essential to psychoanalytic praxis. For example, Lacanian practitioners tend to be quite blunt (and seemingly authoritarian in the tone of their instruction): 'Say whatever you want to say ... say especially whatever you would rather not say ... .'

This is concordant with Lacan's aphorism, presented in his *Séminaire* of 1954–1955, that 'there is only one resistance, the resistance of the psychoanalyst.' In passing, we may note that the aphorism is not substantively dissimilar from the argument I have presented several times elsewhere—namely that what curbs and curtails the effectiveness of any psychoanalytic treatment is always the psychoanalyst's narcissism. The Lacanian instruction also exemplifies this school's contention that the method of psychoanalysis should bypass considerations of the patient's ego organization, and it reflects his emphasis on *saying*—that is, the premise that the relation between psychoanalyst and patient is, first and foremost, a *linguistic* relation (I will take issue with this in the next chapter).

In my clinical experience, even the most sophisticated patients begin with little idea how challenging it is to 'say especially what you would rather not say.' In my own training (which was tainted with ego-psychology), something less peremptory, more politely invitational, and compassionately anticipatory of the difficulties that will certainly lie ahead was advocated. Something like:

> Please say out loud whatever comes into your mind—everything that comes into your stream of consciousness—even if it is something about me, something that you ordinarily would not say in someone else's presence, something that makes you uncomfortable, or something that seems irrelevant or nonsensical.

This still entails a double problem. The emphasis on 'saying' and on 'mind' reruns the Lacanian emphasis on linguistics (downplaying or dismissing the embodied meaningfulness of our flesh, blood, and bones). That is, it positions psychoanalysis as a 'talking cure,' which is taken to mean 'the cure is only by talking' (as will be discussed later, this is a formula which needs to be amended). Also, the invitation still sets the patient up for failure. It is impossible to say 'everything that comes into your stream of consciousness.'

Here is a quick experiment: Close your eyes for a few moments and follow your 'stream of consciousness.' I believe you will quickly realize that this 'stream' is far too fast, too multi-levelled, and too polysemous for it to be utterable (except very selectively, which raises questions about how such a selection is being undertaken). Interestingly, although he certainly knew of William James' description, in his masterwork of 1890, of consciousness and life itself as a 'stream,' Freud used the term only briefly. In his writings, it seems solely to appear in a 1901 essay where he writes about *der ungehemmte Fluß der Assoziationen* (the 'uninhibited flow of a stream of associations'). But then, significantly, he seems to drop the notion of *Fluß*, coming to prefer the images of a line, thread, train, or chain (*Linie, Faden, Zug, Verkettung*). There is something useful about the notion of a *chaining* of associations, since each item may be very different from those which come before and after, yet they are linked, even if the meaning of the linkage is not evident (because the link is a matter of condensation and displacement, metaphor and metonym).

To return to the issue of facilitating the patient's free-association, there are a number of aspects that require presentation and sometimes repeated discussion with the patient. In my psychoanalytic practice, I have arrived at something like the following:

> As your part in our journey together, I invite you to try to utter whatever occurs in your mind and whatever occurs in your body—even if it is something you would not ordinarily express aloud in someone else's presence, such as something about me, or even if it is something that makes you uncomfortable, such as something you consider abhorrent or shameful, or even if it is something that seems irrelevant or nonsensical in relation to whatever is happening in our session. I do understand this is very challenging to accomplish. So, when we come to moments in which it seems to you to be impossible to utter something out loud—as I am sure we will—we can discuss together why it seems to you that some matters are difficult to allow yourself to express.

The main problem with this version is that it is lengthy, and thus usually too challenging for patients to assimilate all at once. It also postpones my encouraging patients to be as physically comfortable as possible, and to close their eyes while free-associating. Different aspects of the invitation usually have to be gently reiterated and clarified in the course of the treatment. This is especially true of 'whatever occurs in your body' because, especially in eurocentric cultures, patients are quite accustomed to living at a little distance from the sensual movements of their embodiment (more about this will be elaborated later). Accordingly, the reason for using words like 'utter' and 'express'—instead of 'say' and 'speak'—is that noises and bodily events, such as a burp, a yawn, a momentary pain or a muscular twitch are to be welcomed into the discourse, even as the patient is lying comfortably prone with eyes closed (this will also be elaborated later). Finally, from my standpoint, it is important that the phrasing sets a collaborative tone to the psychoanalyst-patient relationship, with an indirect indication that the psychoanalyst's main role—aside from remaining silent and allowing patients timespace in which to listen to themselves as they express utterances into what is, in a fundamental sense, a deathful void—will be to address the patient's resistances to free-association so that they can eventually be appreciatively relinquished or dissolved.

There is, of course, nothing magically determinative about the wording by which a psychoanalyst facilitates the patient's entering into the treatment process (although there are definitely several ways in which this may be done counterproductively). Perhaps the various phrasings just indicated are as important for psychoanalysts to hear themselves say out loud to the patient as they are for the latter to gradually assimilate. That is, the articulation of the *Grundregel* poignantly but indirectly reminds the practitioner that the silence of the psychoanalyst is ultimately of far greater service to the patient than producing interpretations (which is doing psychotherapy rather than psychoanalysis). But what is at issue eventually is the way in which free-association is to be engaged. We can now come to crucial questions about the method's character and conditions.

A heuristic illustration

So imagine you are now sitting in a quiet, private setting with a person called a patient. You know he is your patient because he is taking care of you; he sustains your livelihood by paying you every month 1/10th to 1/30th of your living expenses (depending on how many patients you see in a week). We will call him a patient because in some way he knows he is suffering, and he has described to you an ailment suitable for psychoanalytic treatment (the important notion of an ailment, contrasted with concepts such as symptom, formulated assessment, or diagnosis was discussed in my *What is Psychoanalysis?*). 'Patient' comes from the Latin meaning someone who suffers (whereas 'client' comes from a medieval term for someone who pays for legal advice). We will call this patient 'he' (accepting that 'he' could be any of several gender designations), simply for convenience and because the patient I am about to describe happens to be a cis-gendered male. The patient is lying comfortably such that you are out of sight (and in any event, he has been encouraged to keep his eyes closed for the duration of the session). You have issued the 'fundamental rule' in some form as discussed above.

What happens next? I will describe the beginning minutes of a Monday session with my patient that occurred sometime in the second year of treatment. For reasons that will become clear in Chapter Five, I consider any sort of recording or note-taking to violate the fundamental principles of psychoanalysis. So what follows is—necessarily—reconstructed from my memory. In order not to get entirely lost, let me start (and note that a 'starting point' cannot be anything but arbitrary) by telling you what I recall about the ending of the previous Friday's session, which was several days into a new month.

Our agreement was that the patient was to pay for a month of sessions on or before the day of the last session of that month (handing me the payment in person, cash or cheque). The end of the previous month had come and gone, and this Friday session came on the 5th day of the new month, and the patient had repeatedly forgotten to make the payment. In terms of my inner reactions to this enactment, I was not concerned that I would not get paid; I had enough money to meet my bills that month, and I was sure the patient would eventually pay me. But I was alert to his forgetting and regarded his action (or inaction) with a sort of bemused or amused curiosity. It occurred to me that he was perhaps unwittingly performing some sort of unconscious hostility towards me (although it could also be a coercive attempt to have me offer him free appointments out of my affection for him). However, there had been little or no explicit evidence of such feelings in terms of the manifest contents of the week of sessions. His possible hostility did not bother me in the slightest, not least because I sensed that it was associated with, or a reaction against, the possibility of warm affectionate feelings—perhaps homoerotically flavoured—that had persisted between the two of us for several previous months.

So, towards the end of the session, I said to the patient—in what I believe was a light-hearted and equanimous tone—something like: 'Perhaps you are repeatedly forgetting my payment as a way of showing us how difficult it is for you to acknowledge consciously any negative feelings toward me.' For now, let us not fret about whether what I said was a 'good-enough' intervention because what is always important is what follows. The patient's immediate response was as light-hearted as my intervention: 'No, no, no.' Then chuckling, he added 'you're always harping on about things in our relationship being so *significant* … as if you have to do with everything, including the sinking of the Titanic.' And he said goodbye, and left.

As you are unfamiliar with this patient and my relationship with him, I need to pause to explain his mention of the Titanic, which refers to a joke we shared previously and also alludes to our both being Jewish. Two men, one Chinese and the other Jewish-American, are seated together on a long train journey. They are chatting and really enjoying each other's company. Eventually, the Jewish guy observes that it is great they are getting along so well, especially given the bombing of Pearl Harbor. 'Pearl Harbor!' the Chinese guy objects a little indignantly; 'that was the Japanese, not the Chinese.' The American responds, 'Ah yes, but Chinese, Japanese, what's the difference …' Their conversation continues amiably, but a little while later, the Chinese man observes 'you know it really is remarkable how well we are getting along, especially when you consider the sinking of the Titanic …' The Jewish-American man is perplexed, 'the sinking of the Titanic!' he protests, '… the Jews had nothing to do with that!' 'Ah well,' responds the other, 'Greenberg, Grossberg, Iceberg, what's the difference …'

So now the first four 'moments' of Monday's session:

#The patient got onto the couch, his body seeming to fidget uneasily as he did so, and then announced that he had felt 'on edge' all weekend. He did not know why. Next he reflected that he remembered nothing about Friday's session, which he found puzzling.

#He then reported that his pubescent son had seemed angry with him almost all weekend. Eventually, he felt unable to cope with the boy's hostility and left the boy to spend a few hours at his favourite bar.

#He then says 'I have no idea why this is coming to mind right now. I am feeling tight in my chest, and I just had an image of Rabbi B who tutored me for my Bar Mitzvah. I have not thought about him in years.' I internally recalled that the ritual coincided with his Father's illness, which proved terminal. The patient then describes how he had become close to this Rabbi, but at one point he had become angry at the man over some slight or disappointment that he could not now remember. It seemed that the Rabbi had not responded well to this, and thereafter seemed to distance himself from their relationship, eventually disappearing from the patient's life.

#Suddenly, the patient says something like 'Wow!' or 'Oh my goodness! I just realized I had a dream last night … I hadn't remembered it until now.' The recollected dream is a fragment. He and 'a big man, rather like you' are walking in some luscious countryside, perhaps arm-in-arm, as if we were 'bosom buddies.'

We are less than 15 minutes into the session, but for the purposes of this illustration this is enough—although I do need to add a little more detail about my own inner reactions to the extent that I was aware of them and am able to reconstruct and report them. I felt only curiosity about his agitation at the beginning of the session, especially when he signalled that it was connected in some way to our Friday session, which had succumbed to his amnesia. I also did not immediately recall much of what had happened on Friday, and I only remembered the missing fee payment a few minutes later. Then, as he told the story of his son, I felt a momentary inclination to console him—counsel him about how difficult 12-year-old boys can be, warn him about the risks of resorting to alcohol as medication for upset feelings, and so on. All these inclinations to become a counsellor, I censored, keeping silent. Then, as the son story progressed and just before the patient moved to the story of the Rabbi, I recall feeling a sort of shallowing of my breath, which I took to be as anticipatory anxiety expressed through my thoracic cavity (and this came before the patient reported feeling 'tight' in his chest). As the Rabbi story came to its ending, my bodily sensations moved to a warm feeling in my abdomen (and a deepening or relaxing of my breath) just as the memory of the dream arrived. Of course, in addition to the awareness of my bodily sensation and emotions, I was also, inevitably and to some minor extent, engaged in what one might call ratiocinative or cogitative 'thinking'—figuring out 'what's what'—about the patient's associations. That is, behaving to some small degree as if I were a psychotherapist. But it seems important to note here that, the more I have grown as a psychoanalyst, the less

I think like that when listening to my patients. Rather, I think mostly to deconstruct my own inner reactions as I listen to the patient.

For the purposes of this illustration, let us now try to take apart the sequencing of the patient's speech-acts. I assume it can be agreed that, in his opening, the patient signals—by way of reporting his amnesia for the Friday's session—that his feeling 'on edge' over the weekend is linked to the events of Friday. This does not diminish the fact that the interactions with his son are, in and of themselves, important.

So, if we now consider, at least crudely, the narratological significance of the report of the events with his son. The story has two moments: The son seems hostile to the patient, and the patient leaves for a bar. In the first moment, the son is the actor, there is affect-action (hostility), and the recipient of it is the patient. In the second moment, the patient is the actor, there is affect-action (leaving), and the recipient of it is the son. *Hoc illud est quod est*—the story is what it is, but it also isn't just what it is. Taking it for what it appears to be, we can easily hear the contingency between the two moments: The positions of actor/recipient are reversed, and the affect-action of antagonism leads to the affect-action of abandonment. We must also note—in terms of the ways in which the present is always constituted by a medley of 'past-futures' (which will be discussed later)—that this story is framed as occurring in the recent past, quite proximate to the present discourse between the patient and myself.

Next comes the narration of the Rabbi story, again with two contingent moments: The patient was angry with the Rabbi, and the Rabbi distanced himself, later disappearing. In the first moment, the patient is the actor, there is affect-action (anger), and the recipient of it is Rabbi B. In the second moment, the Rabbi is the actor, there is affect-action (distancing-departure), and the recipient of it is the patient. Again, *hoc illud est quod est*—the story is what it is, but it also isn't just what it is. Taking it for what it appears to be, we can hear the contingency between the two moments: The positions of actor/recipient are reversed, and the affect-action of anger leads to the affect-action of distancing and departure. Again, we should note that this story is framed as occurring in the distant, almost forgotten past—seemingly quite temporally remote in relation to the present discourse between the patient and myself.

If we take the two stories together, the patient is recipient and then actor (he receives the son's anger, then leaves to go drinking), followed by actor and then recipient (he is angry at Rabbi B, then has to receive the latter's distancing and subsequent departure from the relationship). However, the contingency of affect-action is constant: The expression of hostility or anger leads to abandonment. Moreover, the timeframe shifts from being marked as chronologically close to the present conversation to being quite temporarily distant from the participants in the current discourse. Yet we must also note that the more distant story is also more dire (at least at the time): The Rabbi's discontinuation of the relationship seems more drastic than the intermission for a few hours that the patient imposed upon his son.

In passing, although not the primary purpose of this illustration, the discussion thus far points up the fallacy of treating any particular story—any manifest content—as if its meaning were not, in some profound but hidden sense, dependent upon, and to be elucidated by, what comes before it and what comes after it. Counsellors and coaches inevitably have to treat manifest contents in this manner. That is, they engage with the manifest contents as they are in and of themselves. Consider the temptation I had when listening to the son story to move out of my psychoanalytic position and intervene (to console him, counsel him, empathize about how difficult 12-year-old boys can be, warn him about the risks of resorting to alcohol as medication for upset feelings, and so on). Psychotherapists (at least those who are psychoanalytically-oriented) do not counsel. Rather, they intervene interpretively on the basis of what they hear as the linkages, the latent themes, that are evident in the movement from one story to the next. For example, 'it seems that, in your mind, angry feelings tend to disrupt or destroy relationships.' So, if a clinician's wish is to move from being a counsellor or coach to being a psychotherapist, here is a useful aphorism: If you give weight to any particular item of manifest content, you may end up doing beneficial counselling, but a psychoanalytically-oriented psychotherapist does not give too much credence to what is heard in the presentation of manifest contents, but rather tries to hear the significance of the shifts from one manifest content to another, which indicate the emergence of latent—suppressed—themes. We will soon return to this point.

So, what of the dream that is suddenly recalled and reported immediately after the sequence of manifest contents (from son story to Rabbi story)? Now the patient and a person who seems to represent the psychoanalyst ('a big man, rather like you') are walking in luscious countryside as if 'bosom buddies.' The patient added something like 'arm-in-arm,' but interestingly, when I first came to review and write about the session as I remembered it, I made a slip and thought 'hand-in-hand,' which seems, in my mind, a degree more romantic-erotic.

In passing, we might note that there is the serious mistake that many psychotherapists make—in their impatience to arrive at interpretations—by responding to dreams in terms of their manifest content. All too easily one can hypothesize: Luscious countryside refers to the maternal body; a 'bosom' is not only about breasts but is the chest, which is figuratively the source of emotion; a 'buddy' is a comrade or pal but also often a term of endearment; 'arm-in-arm' (or 'hand-in-hand') suggests a romantic connection, perhaps with an erotic implication. These ideas may well be relevant. However, at this point they are my associations, and I am not going further with how the patient continued after he had disclosed the manifest content of the dream (although obviously my translation of arm-in-arm to hand-in-hand indicates the arousal of my countertransference in some way).

Rather than go further, for the purposes of this illustration, we should merely note how the reporting of the manifest dream modifies the patient's prior speech-acts in at least three ways. The relation of actor/recipient is abolished, as is the contingency of affect-action (in which hostility seems to issue into abandonment). Moreover, the timeframe of the story changes from the recent or remote past to the liminal temporality of dreams, which is a strange past-and-future (past in that the dream images refer to previous experiences, future in that the dream bespeaks wishes).

So, we can now understand more deeply—psychotherapeutically—*both* what happened at the end of Friday's session in terms of the first few minutes of Monday's session, *and* vice versa. Friday's session concluded with me saying 'perhaps your repeatedly forgetting to pay me indicates how difficult it is for you to acknowledge negative feelings toward me,' to which he responded first with denial and then by teasing me with the Titanic joke. Given how he picks up this issue on Monday, it seems that, whereas the patient *consciously* hears me saying that he might have some hostility towards me, what he hears *unconsciously* (in the sense of a latent or suppressed theme) is something like 'if I experience or express hostile feelings towards Barnaby, he will abandon me.' The associational sequence on Monday riffs on this theme. The patient even signals, right at the start of the session, that he is reacting to something that occurred on Friday, when he announces both his edginess over the weekend and his being puzzled that he could remember nothing about Friday's session.

It needs to be emphasized that understanding the sequencing of the patient's material in this way does not invalidate the meaning of each item in and of itself. The manifest content of each item is indeed one 'channel' of communication, but not the only one. A well-meaning counsellor will engage with such contents, but a good-enough psychotherapist (by which I mean a competent and psychoanalytically-oriented one) will not engage with a manifest item, even while respecting its significance to the patient in and of itself. Rather, such a clinician tries to hear the latent thematics, and then interpret them for the patient's benefit, telling him something about himself of which he seems not to be conscious (in that he does not himself reflectively articulate the theme). There are several interventions that a good-enough psychotherapist might appropriately make at the end of the sequence. To give just three examples: 'When I spoke on Friday of your difficulty acknowledging negative feelings toward me, you reacted in terms of your conviction that negative feelings in a relationship portend its ending …' or 'You want us to be bosom buddies and partly this is because you are scared that negative feelings will upset or destroy our relationship …' or 'It was important that you forgot my fee last week as a way of sharing your negative feelings towards me because in your mind any more direct expression of them would have led to my dumping you …' All of these examples are probably too long-winded to be optimally useful to the patient (that is, to be heard and assimilated by him). However, such interventions, each with their pros and cons in terms of wording, tact, and timing, do constitute good-enough psycho-*therapy*.

However, they are *not* inherently the function of a psycho-*analyst*, except in the initial psychotherapeutic phase of a psychoanalytic treatment—the phase that I indicated typically lasts at least a year before a truly psychoanalytic process gets underway.

So, there is more. Going beyond psychotherapy, there is an additional dimension that is difficult to grasp for anyone who has not entered into a genuinely psychoanalytic process (that is, going beyond the hunt for latent themes that might be beneficially interpreted). Allow me to point to a dimension that is *otherwise* than the *other* themes that can sooner or later be represented and interpreted accordingly. This is a dimension that, in the next chapter, I will characterize as deeply recondite and energetic. That is, a dimension the manifestation and awareness of which are quite specific to the healing properties of a commitment to ongoing free-associative discourse. For the sake of illustration, consider the following.

After the opening of Monday's session (in which the patient's body fidgeted as he got uneasily onto the couch and announced both his 'edginess' and his amnesia for the Friday session), there is a poetic rhythm of what I will call subtle energies. It is expressed in his going to a *bar*, remembering a *Bar* Mitzvah tutored by Ra*bb*i *B*, and then being *B*osom *B*uddies. All of this is spoken to a psychoanalyst named *Bar*naby *B* *Bar*ratt. I ask: Is there not a deeper dimension here, one that intimates an excess of meaningfulness in an energetic momentum, which is not to be captured representationally, yet which flows dynamically between me and the patient? The phonemic rhythm of the letter *B* points to a dimension of traces that works-and-plays ('workplays') around bodily erotics and the persistence of death (or what should be called the 'deathfulness of life itself' as suggested by a rereading of Freud's infamous 1920 essay in which he introduces the notion of *Todestrieb*).

Deathfulness is intimated by the watery depths into which the Titanic sank, in the life-and-death struggle into which patriarchal culture inevitably throws sons with their fathers or father-figures. This is betokened by the patient, who performs the mythic role of the emblematic Father who suicides in response to the Son's patricidal ambitions. It is betokened by the Rabbi as an emblem of patriarchal fatherhood, and by an actual Father, who died around the time of the patient's symbolic entry into manhood, his Bar Mitzvah. Finally, it is betokened by the notion of Bosom Brotherhood, which abolishes the mythic to-the-death conflict between Fathers and Sons. Bosom Brotherhood points to an erotic bliss whimsically traversing the maternal body and pointing—as erotics always do—to life beyond death as the *terminus ad quem*, as when life is asserted into the orgasmic momentum of 'le petit mort.' This recondite momentum intimates a profusion of energies that is not reducible or translatable into representation.

The difference between soft (story-telling) and radical (full-on) free-association

We can now confront the crucial question of the way in which—or the extent to which—the method of free-association conforms to and yet, to a greater or lesser degree, transgresses the narratological imperative. This also sharpens the distinction between free-association being deployed as a data-gathering technique towards interpretation, which is its epistemological use, and the method being appreciated foremost as a remobilization of the patient's being-becoming, which I am calling its *ontoethical* engagement (more on this in my Concluding note).

Before going further with this distinction, I must express my homage to the anglophone writings of Anton Kris and of Christopher Bollas, despite the fact that I am about to raise critical questions about their different standpoints. Selecting their landmark contributions is not intended to dishonour the contributions of others—here, along with Torsti-Hagman, one might mention papers by Mark Kanzer, Patrick Mahony, Savo Spacal, and others that I have previously mentioned. Nietzsche suggested that one repays a teacher poorly if one remains a student. Generally, it may be that without intelligent contributions such as those of Kris and Bollas the topic of free-association might have disappeared entirely from serious consideration by the large segment of the 'psychoanalytic' community that is not devoted to Lacanian teachings. Specifically, the clarity of their writings has stimulated my understanding of the ways in which their standpoints are to be appreciated critically but taken radically further. One learns from teachers the ways in which one must diverge from their teachings.

A close reading of Kris' eminent and influential essay hints at confusion about—yet ultimately a clear commitment to—the epistemological usage of free-association as technique. He argues that 'the central point in psychoanalysis is the commitment to the free-association method,' and at times it seems that the 'goal' of psychoanalytic treatment is solely the enhancement and expansion of the patient's spontaneous capacity to free-associate at will (which implies a function quite different from that of data-gathering). Yet this is undercut by many passages in which it seems the purpose of the method is to provide material for interpretation. The issue hangs rather paradoxically in his text. The former hints that the method itself is changeful, yet Kris' implicit determination to locate psychoanalytic treatment as a science (in the analytico-referential or logical-empiricist sense) ultimately compels him to see free-association as technique. In short, he is writing about the soft version of free-association that ultimately prioritizes the epistemological value of the method over its potential to mobilize our being-becoming.

Bollas' writings on diverse topics render him perhaps one of the most eminent, provocatively thoughtful and consistently interesting psychoanalysts at the turn of this century. His commitment to free-association seems unswerving, and he provides us with one of the best expositions of what I am calling the soft version of this method. Indeed, books such as his 2002 *Free Association*, and his 2009 publications, *The Evocative Object World* and *The Infinite Question*, as well as subsequent works (perhaps most notably, *The Mystery of Things* and *The Freudian Moment*), have had a significant impact in countering the contemporary marginalization (or outright dismissal) of Freud's method. His beautifully illustrated dedication to this method seems ultimately to operate towards an *aesthetics of making sense* (perhaps distinguished herein from the ontoethical value of 'unsaying' or not making sense, unmaking sense). For him, free-association seems less like a frantic epistemological project, more like a way of living aesthetically. It is appreciated as such a practice of expanding self-consciousness through the promotion of intimacy, freedom, and safety, yet adhering comparatively closely to the narratological imperative (and hence ultimately committed to 'making sense'). It is this emphasis—story-telling more as an aesthetics for living, than as an epistemological tool by which to arrive at alleged certainties—that makes Bollas' writings on soft free-association so evocatively compelling.

Bollas defines free-association as 'uncensored talking.' This is significant, not only because 'talking' would seem to emphasize the conveyance of thoughts, feelings, wishes, and fantasies in spoken language (although I do not think Bollas should be charged with prioritizing the constative over the performative). The phrasing is also significant because 'lack of censorship' may be too weak a term for what the process of free-association can potentially invite into expression (which is the argument for a more radical approach that appreciates the deconstructive potency of the method). Indeed, grasping free-association merely as the absence of censorship may curtail or foreclose the potential for a more full-on—ontoethically impactful—experience of these processes. From his 2002 publication, here is an example of what Bollas illustrates as his understanding of the method:

> … I might start my walk to work thinking about a bill I must be sure to pay that afternoon when I'm at my office; then think about the rainfall and wonder if the sun will come out today; then think about a friend's newly published book which I haven't read and feel I should before we meet for dinner next week; then think about my early schooldays as I see children being dropped off at the nearby school; then think about how worried one could get as a child about being on time for school; then, on sight of a few sparrows flying by, think about the spring and wonder if they are now nesting; then think of the phrase 'nest eggs' …

Several aspects of this example may be noted, the most important of which is that each item makes sense in and of itself, conforming to the narratological imperative. Along with that, there is little or no evidence of the voicing of embodied experience. The consequence is that, in Bollas' example, one can scarcely get a sense of the subterranean rhythm of sensuality-sexuality and deathfulness, which was illustrated quite starkly with my patient. This is especially noteworthy because in this essay I am arguing that the more the narratological imperative is relinquished, the greater the intimation of an unrepresentable—repressed—movement of meaningfulness within us.

Bollas is focused on free-association as a sequence of telling stories, each of which makes sense, but the sequencing of which is unconsciously governed by latent—suppressed—themes. As indicated in my example, this makes for good psychotherapy but limits the psychoanalytic potential of the discourse. It is also clear that Bollas' idea of the method is such that it can be undertaken while taking a walk and without the presence of a qualified psychoanalyst (which is much less the case for more full-on or radical free-association). Indeed, the burden of Bollas' 2002 essay is to suggest that all people are free-associating all the time. In his opinion, it is 'an ordinary part of everyday thinking' except for its clinical utility as 'uncensored talking.' He suggests that the virtue of the clinical situation is that it highlights the sequencing of stories—the transitioning from one to the next discloses the latent thematics of self-conscious thought processes. In his terminology, it brings the 'unthought known' into thought. It seems there is little, if any, room in his thinking for the voicing of repressed forces that are unrepresentable—the possibility that the chaining of free-associations opens discourse to otherwise forces that are anti-narratological yet are the energetic force of our being-becoming.

Radicalizing free-association implies that the subject allows a greater latitude of transgression in relation to the rules and regulations of making sense—allowing the expression of a dimension of meaningfulness that violates, or eludes, the narratological imperative. Here is an example from a cis-gendered female patient in her third year of psychoanalysis using the couch. She is doing something more like babbling the 'stream' of consciousness in a way that I cannot possibly reproduce (but will try to sketch from my memory, in order to exemplify more full-on processes of free-association):

> … miserable fuck Robin *prick!* … limp dick Sanile dickhead … beautiful sexy hibiscus … cunt warm now … Lawrence's questing bitch … *ouch!* womb pain bad back …

Of course, this illustration is additionally artificial in that it omits my reactions and responses as I listened to this material. Also, on the basis of her treatment with me, I could tell you much about this patient: How she is married to Sanile, a younger man, whom she finds sexually inept; how her current secret lover, Robin, occasionally seems only a little less so; how she is fascinated by the flower of the Chinese Hibiscus (*Hibiscus rosa-sinensis* with its red or pink petals surrounding a showy stamen fused into a central tube around the pistil); how she usually speaks of 'cunt' as her vagina and 'warmth' as its excitement; how she has been enthralled by a story, written by DH Lawrence around 1924 or 1925 ('The Woman Who Rode Away'), in which a woman goes on a spiritual quest that ends up with her being held captive and somewhat willingly sacrificed by the priests of an indigenous tribe (ritual rape is also suggested). I could also add how I observed her seeming to experience a sharp but transient back spasm just as she was mentioning a 'questing bitch.' Indeed, in the terminology of literary theorists, we can do a 'reading' of this material—in the terminology of physicists, we can give the material a 'treatment'—but, in a profound sense, the relevance of such epistemological enterprises is dubious at best. Indeed, the problem with producing such a 'reading' is that it takes us in the direction of a potentially psychotherapeutic accomplishment, which psychoanalysis goes beyond—as has been demonstrated.

The epistemological pressure to 'make sense' of my patient's performative process may (or may not) be of interest *after the fact*, but it is profoundly irrelevant to the way in which, in the here and now, the process is opening her being-becoming to a meaningfulness previously suppressed and repressed. My point is that radicalizing the method of free-association, and dropping the insistence that free-association is foremost a means by which to make greater sense of the patient's world (according to some preestablished criteria of epistemology), opens her discourse to a greater awareness of the vitality of repressed but embodied meaningfulness, the movements of psychic energies (within both her 'body' and her 'mind'). Going beyond the mandate to interpret and proceeding from soft to full-on free-association takes the expressiveness of the patient's utterances and bodily sensations towards greater awareness of unrepresentable—repressed—movements of psychic energy. But this awareness is not equivalent to self-reflective representational consciousness (I will return to this in the next chapter).

Obviously, there is something of a ruptured continuum between story-telling free-association and the more radicalized method. But the difference is nonetheless downright crucial.

Soft free-association retains a greater degree of making sense. It complies more with the rules and regulations of the narratological imperative. It is a mode of uncensored talking that speaks out loud the ordinary flow of thinking in stories (whether amplified or abbreviated). It is usually deployed as a technique for gathering information or 'data' about the patient's inner theatre of representations, and thus it is usually acknowledged as one means by which to build towards interpretation—the representational formulation of latent or suppressed themes, which is where psychotherapy rests. Thus, although Bollas' approach seems aesthetic, the use of soft free-association is typically epistemological (bringing the 'unthought known' into the arena of thinking). That is, it aims to know within an analytico-referential or logical-empiricist notion of what it means to know, and thus eventually to be able to represent or formulate something other than the manifest content of meaningfulness—indeed, to do so in a way that is correspondent with its reality, coherent or rational in its implications and ramifications, and pragmatically useful to the life of the subject. But this suppressed 'other' that soft free-association discovers—the latent themes within the movement of manifest contents—is not the *otherwiseness* of the repressed, the being-becoming of which is mobilized more vivaciously by a more radicalized engagement with free-associative praxis.

Full-on or radical free-association not only offends convention but violates the rules and regulations of the narratological imperative. It has greater vitality and seems to exhibit or expose an unrepresentable momentum of psychic energy. This suggests that the secret power of free-association—and the reason that the praxis is necessary for psycho-*analytic* processes to be engaged—lies with the negatively dialectical or deconstructive impact it has upon the system and structure of representationality. The key to its effectiveness is that it opens discourse to what is 'in' the theatre of representation but not 'of' its capacity for representation. It allows the voicing of repressed energies that are neither represented nor representable, and it does so in a way that is less an act of epistemology and more a praxis of ontoethical awareness—opening discourse to what is *there!* Such a praxis is not a technique towards therapeutic interpretation, but rather a changeful method that is itself curative.

Chapter 4

What is this 'unconscious'?

The 'unconscious' is probably one of the most overworked terms in the history of the human sciences, of allopathic medicine, and of philosophy in the euromodern tradition. Arguably, it has become unserviceable and should be dropped.

Neurologically, the 'unconscious' could refer to any operation outside the domain of the cerebral cortex (the occipital cortices and claustrum, including the gating functions of midbrain reticular formation and certain thalamic nuclei). This domain seems to be responsible for *consciousness as self-consciousness* or content-related consciousness—representations that are, or can on reflection become 'I-Now-Is'—meaning that which can be articulated or reported representationally. However, *consciousness as awareness*—meaning the condition of being awake, which can be differentiated from content-related consciousness—involves a larger neural network, so then everything outside of such a network might be characterized definitively as unconscious.

Psychologically, the 'unconscious' could refer to all the mechanisms that underpin the operations of consciousness but are again not-conscious and are never going to be. Examples of this could include mechanisms as diverse as those involved in depth perception, which we deploy without knowing how we are doing so; or syntax, by which we know if a sentence makes sense without being able to specify the rules by which we are making such a determination; or countless other features of our ability to function in the world.

DOI: 10.4324/9781003558262-4

These neurological and psychological phenomena would have been better labelled 'non-conscious,' for the invocation of the term 'unconscious' has greatly confused important issues. It has severely interfered with an appreciation of the distinctiveness of Freud's discoveries. None of these neurological and psychological phenomena are *psychodynamic*. They are not inherently tied to the conflicts and contradictions of our self-consciousness. For example, we have not experienced the operations by which depth perception functions and then subsequently suppressed or repressed the knowledge from the purview of our reflective representationality. Unless we were to suddenly have a hysterical symptom in which we lost the ability to perceive depth, nothing about the mechanisms of this ability is involved in psychodynamic discord. Depth perception is an example of just one of these non-conscious phenomena that are not conflictually or contradictorily unconscious, in the psychodynamic sense of being suppressed or repressed. In a sense, they are existentially irrelevant—by which I mean we do not typically factor them in when we come to explore the meaningfulness of our lived-experience, our positionality within the universe.

As psychodynamic endeavours, psychoanalytically-informed psychotherapy and psychoanalysis are both existential disciplines, in that they concern the meaningfulness of our existence, engaging lived-experience in an adventurous campaign of self-discovery that is committed to truthfulness and the process of freeing ourselves from the internal conditions that constrain or constrict us. But the procedures and processes of these adventures are profoundly different. Psychotherapy transforms the individual's representational system, relieving the detrimental representational formations of suppression, but it does little transmutatively to undo the repressiveness of representationality. In practice, a psychoanalytic treatment starts with psychotherapeutic procedures (that usually take up the first year of the treatment). But then, by radicalizing the method of free-association, it goes further and deeper. The radicalized praxis has a uniquely de-repressive impact, for it distinctively mobilizes being-becoming. Thus, in an ontoethical movement, it goes beyond the procedures of knowing about, beyond elaboration of the constructions of understanding. Appreciating the difference between suppression and repression is thus crucial to grasping the unique significance of free-associative praxis, and indeed of the discipline of psycho-*analysis* itself.

The dynamics of suppression versus repression

Regrettably, some of the most profligate misuses of the term 'unconscious' occur in the professional literature of 'psychoanalysis' exactly where one might imagine that the terminology would be best clarified. Yet here the suppressed or descriptive unconscious is routinely conflated with the unconscious-as-repressed. To be fair, even Freud made this error quite often, perhaps especially after 1914, as the elaboration of theories of mental functioning had the effect of dispelling his earlier notion of psychic energy.

In 1914 and 1915, as he came to the end of two pioneering decades of experimentation with the method of free-association, Freud wrote a series of 'metapsychological papers.' What I am now going to suggest—without doing a scrupulous reading of these papers—is definitely not an orthodox treatment of Freud's ideas, and quite possibly not one that he would have endorsed. I argue that what is centrally important is the way these papers can be read *both* as pointing to the crucially significant distinction between the descriptive unconscious-as-suppressed and the more psycho-*analytically* salient unconscious-as-repressed *and* as offering consequential speculations as to how and why repressive processes occur.

About suppression: As discussed previously in our brief introduction to the doctrine of defence mechanisms, innumerable representations that were once within the purview of our self-consciousness are kept in a condition of suppression (*Unterdrückung*). The condition may be—so to speak—deep or shallow, and conflictual to a greater or lesser degree. Consider here some mundane examples: What I ate for dinner last night (which I can quite easily recall); what happened in Friday's session (which my male patient knows that he cannot readily remember); the names of your teachers in elementary school (which you might be able to recollect if you thought about it for a while); my first lover's telephone number (which I definitely cannot recall but which I might recognize and reappropriate if someone told it to me with a sort of 'Oh, yes, that sounds right' reaction). All these representations are variously suppressed from the immediacy of reflective self-consciousness. They are somehow 'stored in memory' and, under certain conditions, it seems they can return to—or be retrieved in and reappropriated by—reflective self-consciousness.

However, it must be emphasized that the notion of memory as storage must never be taken to imply that, while out of consciousness, a representation persists—somehow preserved more or less pristinely in its originally experienced state. That is, maintained like a photograph consigned to your basement archive—an imagistic representation that may fade but which accurately retains its basic features.

Everyone accepts that the present is determined by the past that happened. For example, my experiences with my current lover are shaped both by many previous experiences of lovers and others. This is the *historicity* of lived-experience. The present is also shaped by pasts that did not happen, which is the consideration of 'hauntology'—a perspective that has only very recently come into psychoanalytic consideration, and which is too complex to address at this juncture. The present is also determined by my memories of those previous experiences. This is the *historicality* of lived-experience. Historicity and historicality interact in ways that make the determination of the present by the past dauntingly convoluted. Everyone acknowledges something about these ways in which the past shapes our present—even if we do not know what to do with them to whatever extent we may be conscious of them, let alone how to escape the past's pathways of determination.

However, our sense of ourselves tends to protest the tenet that every memory is reconstructed, and distortedly so. We want to believe that we can remember at least some things 'just the way they were'—as if there were indeed snapshots immaculately conserved in the basement. However, a retrieved or recognized memory that is 'about the past' is always coloured, warped, and twisted by the influence of present conditions. A memory never returns an event to consciousness 'just the way it was.' Even my memory of a strikingly colourful bird that flew past my window just a few minutes ago cannot now be recalled 'just the way it was'—unwittingly, I have already revised and indeed re-revised the representation. This way in which our memories of the past are ineluctably distorted by the present tends to offend our sense of the cogency, coherence, and continuity of the world we inhabit.

The ongoing revision of the past by the present is a major Freudian insight into the character and conditions of our psychic realities. Consider his notion of screen memories in which either the recollection of past events is routinely revised so as to hide aspects of those events that were disturbing at that time, or—less commonly—a disturbing aspect of something in the here-and-now is hidden by the creatively revised recollection of an event set in the past. Also to be considered here is Freud's uniquely potent notion of *Nachträglichkeit* (or 'afterwardsness'), in which the memory of an event that was seemingly innocuous at the time subsequently becomes traumatic because of changes in the subject doing the remembering.

It is evident that the processes of suppression are multifarious. The reason that an item has been pushed out of consciousness may be less a matter of conflict (*as if* I said to myself, 'I cannot possibly remember all thirty items on my shopping list' or 'Enough of looking at that beautiful bird that just flew past my window, I must get back to my writing'). The reason may be more clearly marked by the intensity of the conflict ('My neighbour has angered me, and right now I cannot remember his surname, although I know it damn well!'... *as if* I had said to myself, 'Forget his name, I want him dead!'). The degree of suppression may be deeper (my first lover's phone number) or shallower (what I ate for dinner last night), and the issues of conflict and of depth are often, but not necessarily, correlated.

In addition to all these mundane examples of suppression affecting memory, it must be emphasized that every one of what clinicians call 'defence mechanisms' involves suppression. To give just three simple examples: (i) If I am convinced that 'all people from Fredon are vermin,' it can be inferred that I am denying any 'vermin' qualities within myself, suppressing their admission into the purview of my self-consciousness and attributing or projecting them onto the people of Fredon; (ii) Lady Macbeth washes her hands compulsively, even in her sleep, which suppresses and symbolically-enactively expunges her wishes to kill, and it also cleanses her (at least to the extent that the 'damned spot' might be washed out) of responsibility for manipulating others to do a killing on her behalf; (iii) A patient's right leg twitches as he lies on my couch and, through inviting him to free-associate to the event, the thought of his wishing to kick me comes into his reflective self-consciousness (so we can surely infer that the thought was previously suppressed, and then expressed by his twitching muscle).

In all these examples of memory and of defensive mechanisms, the defining feature of suppression is that when a suppressed item returns to, and is reappropriated by, our self-consciousness it does so as a representation (that is 'I-Now-Is'). This is pertinent both for memory and for the interpretation of defence mechanisms. The retrieved or recognized item may be linguistic (Freud's *Wortvorstellung*), imagistic (rather like Freud's *Sachvorstellung* or *Dingvorstellung*), or somatically-enactively encoded (for example, because of a wartime experience of being under fire many years ago, you still duck down reflexively whenever you hear a loud bang), but once it returns to our reflective consciousness it is representational.

This point deserves reiteration: *The return of the suppressed is always in the composed form of a representation.* Although the forms of the return are probably always significantly different from that of the representations that initially succumbed to suppression, they are, as representations, *inter-translatable*. That is, the representation that was suppressed and the representation that was later reappropriated can be translated, one into the other (by condensation and displacement, metaphor and metonym), even though there will always be some loss (as well as addition) of information in the process of translation.

About repression: Freud's notion of repression (*Verdrängung*) is radically different. As mentioned in previous chapters, Freud argued for the existence of a process both more powerful and distinct from that of suppression. When a representation is repressed from our self-consciousness, it is *as if* it crosses a barrier, is decomposed such that it loses its representational form, never to regain it. Thus, between the repressed and the inner theatre of our representations, there is a *failure in translation* (which was Freud's definition of the repression process). That is, once repressed, there is no—adequate—translation back into representational form.

The repressed is untranslatable—that is, not susceptible to recomposition within the law and order of representationality.

This point also deserves reiteration: *The return of the repressed is always as a commotion of psychic energy, and never in the composed form of a representation.* In anticipation of what is to be argued here, we might note that commotions of psychic energy often result from the release of a coagulation of psychic energy that has been held within our erotic embodiment.

Freud articulated his notion of a 'repression-barrier' in the very last years of the 19th century, just when he was articulating his discovery of the way in which the incest taboo impacts the formation of our psychic reality, which is the appropriate way to understand the oedipality of human consciousness (as discussed in my 2019 paper). Although he never formulated his findings quite so explicitly, a close reading of his writings in the years leading up to 1900 leads to the conclusion that *the repression-barrier is formed as the intrapsychic inscription of the incest taboo.* Children's incestuous impulses traumatically shatter their capacity to represent, but the impulses remain, although unthinkable, repressed and yet somatically—energetically—active. I will elaborate this shortly.

What occurs when a thought, wish, feeling, or fantasy loses its representational form, being decomposed even as it is expelled from the purview of our reflective self-consciousness? That is, when—so to speak—it crosses the repression-barrier? The answer is that it becomes a constituent of the dynamic unconscious-as-repressed. If this were not the case—if the constituent 'item' merely ceased to exist or could at some future point be representationally reconstituted (in the way that a suppressed item can be)—there would have been little novelty in Freud's so-called 'discovery of the unconscious.' But the 'item' does not cease to exist. Indeed, Freud was very clear that the repressed both *persists* and *insists.* 'Persistence' means the 'item' never ceases to exist as a constituent of our psychic reality. 'Insistence' means that it is *as if* this constituent is incessantly trying to get back into our inner theatre of representationality, even though it can never do so. Because there is an endless and insuperable failure in translation, unbound energy cannot be contained adequately or sufficiently in the form of representationality. However, this does not mean that the repressed does not impact the representational world.

Rather, it does so as a force that is *otherwise* than representation, as was discussed in my 2017 paper (in the *International Journal of Psychoanalysis*). It impacts the rationality (and the realism) of our inner theatre of representation as a force that is disturbingly disruptive, as if an exuberant excess of 'meaningless meaningfulness.' That is, an exuberant excess of psychic energy that is not bound by its investment in the law and order of representationality. This is surely why one can never understand the dynamic unconscious by means of psychotherapeutic procedures of 'making sense.'

My thesis throughout this essay is that there is only one viable way to consider what happens when a thought, feeling, wish, or fantasy is repressed and thus decomposes, losing its representational form. That is, repressed 'items' persevere as traces—pockets or implants—of psychic energy, which are neither immaterially representational nor materially biological yet are retained as active impulses within the fabric our erotic embodiment.

It can now be appreciated why, in his early publications on psychoanalysis, Freud came to write so emphatically about the repression-barrier. The incest taboo is the 'law of laws,' as is further discussed in my 2015 paper (in the *International Forum of Psychoanalysis*). Our induction into language as a symbolic system positions our subjectivity in relation to the primordial 'no' upon which, as Freud argued, any semblance of civilization depends. The repression-barrier is formed in terms of this primordial demarcation of the forbidden, the unthinkable, or at least that which cannot be experienced-as-a-thought—obviously we can, as adults, think about having contact with our primary caretakers' genitals in an abstractive, affectless sort of way, which is the way in which computers think. However, the concretely arousing sexual impulses, wishes, and fantasies that I experienced excitedly as a toddler in relation to my caretakers' bodies had to be repressed. As soon as I entered into linguistic representationality, such wishes became literally unthinkable in any experiential manner (the symbolic system conveys the primordial 'no'). Yet the impact of my caretakers' erotic relations with me is not expunged but remains deeply encoded in the sensual constitution of my body—recorded as the sexual patterning of energetic traces within my erotic embodiment.

Thus, the consistency of the repressed is that of innumerable traces—pockets, implants, or coagulations—of psychic energy that, in their erotically embodied perseverance, retain something of the 'flavour' of their origin. My use of this notion of 'flavour' points to a certain sort of representationally meaningless meaningfulness. This is a vitally important point to consider. The repressed exists within our sensual embodiment in traces—like little packages—of psychic energy that somehow carry the 'flavour' of what might be called their 'origin' prior to repression.

Sometimes these traces move fluidly within us; sometimes they are more like sticking points, loci of congestion (and thence obstructions to the flow of free-association). In both cases, they are meaningful forces that are not able to be recaptured in representation, yet they disruptively and excessively impact the cogency, coherence, and continuity of our representational functioning.

If the notion of an otherwise mode of meaningfulness being lodged energetically in our sensual embodiment is unfamiliar, then one can think here of the impressive clinical work of somatic healers such as Ron Kurtz, Peter Levine, and Bessel van der Kolk (to name just three). In various ways they show how traumatic experiences (which are by definition those that the representationality of the ego organization cannot process) are recorded in our psychosomatic constitution, our embodied experience. This has been extensively discussed in Michael Heller's 2012 book, as well as in my shorter 2010 introduction, *The Emergence of Somatic Psychology and Bodymind Therapy.*

As Freud came to discuss these issues in his 1915 papers, he realized that the energies of the repressed must be generated in two ways.

First, there are all the traces or pockets of energy that are imposed or imprinted upon us erotically by our caretakers as infants and toddlers (operating preverbally). Such traces or messages never come to be represented yet are constitutive of the sensual patterning of our embodiment. In this respect, they are 'enigmatic,' impressed upon and becoming part of our embodied constitution, without our subsequently developed capacity for representation being able to 'make sense' of them (except by processes of *Nachträglichkeit*). All sensual experiences prior to the establishment of the repression-barrier (the toddler's induction into symbolic language and the installation of the primordial 'no') should therefore be considered as what Freud called the 'originatively repressed' (*Urverdrängung*).

Second, once toddlers have been inducted into their individual place in the linguistic domain, the inchoate representation of forbidden thoughts, feelings, wishes, and fantasies has to be repressed—losing its representational form, as if being pushed into exile beyond the repression-barrier, decomposing into an alive, persistent, and insistent package of energetic traces. This is what Freud called 'actual repression' (*eigentliche Verdrängung*).

Again, the central point here—my thesis—is that Freud's ideas regarding the unconscious-as-repressed, and his distinction between repressive and suppressive processes, ultimately cannot be appreciated or understood unless the notion of subtle energies, pervading the psyche as our erotic embodiment, is invoked. Yet, perhaps remarkably, the notion of such subtle energy systems was not only held ambivalently by Freud but has been routinely disregarded, or supposedly refuted, by all the 'psychoanalysts' who followed him; they have adhered, quite slavishly, to the euromodern masterdiscourse of 'science' that has, by and large, dogmatically ruled out such a notion. The history of 'psychoanalysis' can be read as a history of efforts to expunge the notion of psychic energy, to demote and rhetorically misconstrue the significance of repression, and thus to misunderstand profoundly the unique power of free-associative discourse.

The notion of psychic energy and the not-so-reasonable objections to it

The masterdiscourse that has governed the sciences of the euromodern world, since around the end of the 15th century, has been called that of analytico-referentiality or logical-empiricism. Such sciences have delivered staggering technological advances. Yet, technological success cannot be mistaken as a singular benchmark that is indicative of the truthfulness of reality. As has been discussed extensively within 20th-century philosophy, the masterdiscourse operates on unexaminable metaphysical assumptions. One is that it assumes certain metaphysical binaries, notably material/immaterial and body/mind (which is a scheme that eliminates the notion of subtle or psychic energies). Another is its assumption that if something cannot be scientifically tested—directly observed or inferred logically from the data of some sort of empirical evidence—its existence cannot be ascertained and should even be sceptically denied. And thus, a third assumption is that anything that is real must sooner or later be representable within the rational—mathematizable—law and order of representationality. If there are entities, 'events,' or forces that cannot sooner or later be somehow represented within our thinking and thus are indeed unthinkable they are held to be non-existent. Here one may recall how Georg Hegel, at the pinnacle of euromodern philosophy, published a formula: 'What is rational is real, and the real is rational' (although he used the term 'actual' rather than 'real').

However, in the first two decades of psychoanalytic discovery, Freud was quite devoted to the 'helpful idea' (*Hilfvorstellung*) of psychic energy, although it is a notion that subverts or implodes the metaphysical dichotomy of material/immaterial, and indeed of body/mind. In a 1913 paper and elsewhere, he proposed that psychoanalysis operates in a field or timespace *between* biology and psychology. So we must ask: What can this 'between' (*zwischen*) portend; what can go between the materiality of neurons and the immaterial representationality of the mind? As elaborated in my 2016 book, *Radical Psychoanalysis* and also in my 2022 critique of mind-body dualism, the notion of psychic energy is posed as *neither* material *nor* immaterial yet having an impact or influence on both. So, in a mysterious sense it is *both* material *and* immaterial. It is not fully concordant with the anatomy and physiology known to biologists, even though it may flow within and through such structures and functions. And it is not fully concordant with the inner theatre of representations (thoughts, feelings, wishes, and fantasies) known to psychologists, even though it enters into this system both fuelling its transitions or transformations, and as an excess of meaningfulness, disrupting its cogency, coherence, and continuity (and hence sabotaging its rationalist claims to the totalization of the law and order or representationality).

On some level of his thinking, Freud must have known that his *zwischen*—both the 'between-ness' and the 'within-ness' of subtle energies, *Triebe*, 'desire' or libidinality—did not concord with, and indeed radically indicted, the scientific metaphysics of his time.

On a personal level, he continued to believe in psychic energy for the rest of his life. He privately confided that he had had telepathic experiences, and in 1926 he indicated to Jones that for 'diplomatic' reasons he had not publicized this matter. He then proceeded to tell Jones that his acceptance of telepathy was his 'own affair' and that it had no relevance to psychoanalysis. The latter assertion is, of course, utterly preposterous. If there can be such esoteric and recondite connectivity between thinking minds, then it implies the operation of psychic energies within and outside each individual's mind or brain. That is, the transmission of meaningfulness that is not tied to any demonstrable modality—such as a written inscription, visual perception, or sound wave. This cannot but be operative in every relationship between psychoanalysis and patient and perhaps intensely so with the radicalization of the free-associative praxis (such that subtle and preternatural communications are accentuated).

On a public and professional level, especially after 1914, as Freud came to elaborate his grand theoretical edifices, he kept his notion of psychic energy discreetly sidelined. To some extent it is subsumed under the concept of the sexual and aggressive drives (*Triebe*). However, both within Freud's writing and definitively in all the writings of his followers, these drives are increasingly presented as if logically reducible to the biological dimension of the human condition; for example, as naturally inborn influences generating from the pre-programming of our reptilian brain.

In a sense Freud may himself have betrayed the radical significance of his own notion of *anlehnung* (atrociously translated by Strachey as 'anaclisis'). This is his insight that the *Treibe*—drives that are energetic forces—are not to be equated with their biological substrate, but rather lean on, are propped upon, or are derived from the mechanisms of biology (the instinctual programmes generated within the brainstem and cerebellum). To mention Laplanche's favourite example: Oral libido develops from the innately programmed sucking reflex but is then independent—as an energetic momentum—from this biological mechanism.

Not only can the history of euromodern science be read in terms of efforts to expel and expunge prevalent medieval beliefs in a mystical 'spirit world' that defies logical and empirical proof. But the past century of mainstream psychoanalytic theorizing can similarly be read as a history of various efforts to discard the notion of psychic energy (of course, there are a few notable exceptions, of which Phil Mollon's 2008 *Psychoanalytic Energy Psychotherapy* is eminent). Sometimes the term is preserved nominally as a shorthand for the biological forces of 'drive'—more often it is dispensed with entirely. Such efforts supposedly recast the discipline as if resting on wholly rationalist foundations (within the analytico-referential or logical-empiricist framework) and imply that treatment can be conducted in a fully rational manner (bringing unruly forces under the governance of a lawfully ordered mind or representational system). Thus, Freud's followers, and to a significant extent Freud himself, have ignored the way in which the notion of psychic energies, as remobilized in free-associative discourse, indicts and undermines the metaphysical assumption of a rational/irrational dichotomy.

Let us briefly consider two contemporarily influential versions of 'psychoanalysis' that have theoretically eliminated the 'between-and-within' notion of psychic energy: neuropsychoanalytic theory and Lacanian theory.

Against neuropsychoanalysis: Neuropsychoanalysis has become fashionable in recent decades and, by bringing neuroscience to bear on psychotherapeutic practice, has embarked significantly on an attack against the existential priority of genuinely psychoanalytic praxis. It has justified itself because it purports to be 'hard science,' and it has promoted itself philosophically by appealing to the 'dual-aspect monism' adumbrated in Baruch Spinoza's *Ethics*. The latter was published in 1677 and is considered a landmark in euromodern philosophy. Neuropsychoanalysts deploy a tendentious misreading of this text (see my 2022 paper in Mills' anthology) in order to justify a dubious, and pre-eminently unbalanced, 'marriage' between psychoanalytically-informed psychotherapy and neuroscience. Despite the protests of neuropsychoanalysts that the relationship is two-way, in practice their discipline believes it should dictate the conduct of psychotherapy, and not vice versa. Yet Spinoza held that brain and mind are ontologically different aspects or attributes of *one* substance. This is taken by neuropsychoanalysts as justification for their quirky interpretation of William Whelwill's notion of 'consilience,' which implies that whatever general conclusions are drawn from particular empirical facts about one aspect must agree with conclusions drawn about the other aspect.

'Consilience' is then taken to imply a reductionism that is not only empirical, which holds that immaterial mental events depend on their housing within a system of physical events that are material (notably brain functions), which is a position that many or most people might affirm. However, in neuropsychoanalytic texts, it is also—rather surreptitiously and in a way that is quite flawed intellectually—taken to imply a reductionism that is logical. This means that one set of events must be *intertranslatable* with the other (a position that is quite contrary to Spinoza's ideas about the two aspects or attributes). As just mentioned, these texts are often strident in their insistence that neuropsychoanalysis supposedly does not imply that neuroscientific findings are superior to those of psychotherapy. However, in practice this insistence is merely astute rhetoric serving the political ends of concealing a hegemony. This is because the neuro side is 'hard,' technological science (concordant with the metaphysics of analytico-referentiality or logical-empiricism), whereas psychotherapeutic and psychoanalytic ideas are 'soft.' Thus, with so-called neuropsychoanalysis, conclusions about brain functioning come to dictate how the existential praxis of a healing discourse should be conducted. This exemplifies the hegemonic violence of 'science' in the euromodern era. Allegedly the aggregation of 'hard data' trumps the psychoanalysis of lived-experience (and establishes itself in an imperial position against much else additionally, as will be indicated shortly).

'Hegemonic violence' may seem like a strong indictment, but like many of the 'new' schools of 'psychoanalysis' before it—that produced theoretical models of the mind that are entirely about representationality—neuropsychoanalysis actually disposes entirely of the need for a notion of psychic energy. This jettisoning is sometimes announced blatantly, sometimes undertaken stealthily. Within neuropsychoanalysis, the conceptual expulsion is somewhat obscured—misleadingly—by the neuroscientific endorsement of a mathematical 'free-energy' model of brain functioning, which has been advanced by Karl Friston and others in the recent past. This is a brilliant (but entirely hypothetical) model of the interactive pathways and feedback loops that might pertain between the lower and higher functions of brain activity. In the sense that we are considering psychic energy, Friston's model is not about energy at all; it is what he rather grandly dubs 'a mathematics of the mind.'

A final point that must be made about the neuropsychoanalytic inherent effort to preclude Freud's early notion about the betweenness (and within-ness) of psychic energy. That is, to trivialize such a notion as hocus-pocus ('we do not need murky energy concepts' as one senior colleague blithely informed me). The point is that the neuropsychoanalytic 'take' on Spinoza is bogus. Contrary to the presentation of his ideas made by many neuroscientists, Spinoza never discounted the possibility that there might be other aspects or attributes of the 'one substance' besides those of the materiality of the physical and the immateriality of the representational. This keeps open the possibility of a 'third'—such as psychic energy that passes both within and through the two aspects that are most apparent. Also, Spinoza argues that these attributes of the monistic 'substance' are its expressions, but not in the sense of their properties of predicative formations—the intertranslatability of logical reductionism that is assumed by neuropsychoanalysts is thus actually ruled out by his thesis.

Contrary to the reading of Spinoza on which the hegemony of neuropsychoanalysis pivots, Spinoza's notion of a universal and indivisible 'one substance' does offer some useful points of engagement with the psychoanalytic notion of psychic energy; one example of which would be Gilles Deleuze and Félix Guattari's discussion of the 'planes' of immanence or expressionism. It also engages with the cosmology of indigenous cultures and Asian spirituality, as will be shortly mentioned again. A meaningful force that operates otherwise than the law and order of both biology and psychology is entirely plausible.

Against Lacanianism: The Lacanian school emerged both in the wake of Ferdinand de Saussure's influential lectures on the character and conditions of signs (presented from 1906 to 1911) and also following Roman Jakobson's structuralist approach to linguistics (especially his 1956 paper on the metaphoric and metonymic poles of representation as determining the selective and combinative possibilities of ostensible meaningfulness). The motif of the Lacanian reformulation of Freud's psychology is the relations between signifiers, and the network of signifiers as being a—more or less absolute—totality. There is no possible access to any signified (meaningfulness or 'reality' outside the system of signification), so all meaning (which, breaking with his early interest in surrealism and existentialism, is not a term that Lacan himself favoured) is derived from the multiple chaining of signifiers, in which each signifier conveys a meaning only in terms of its relations with a network of other signifiers (the possible pathways of signifiers are pre-determined).

To introduce this theorizing very briefly: The network of signifiers is ultimately a synchronic totality—the 'register' of the 'Symbolic Order'—which is a structuralist notion and the *sine qua non* of Lacan's ambition to reformulate Freud's discipline. The symbolic order (which is more or less equivalent to the way in which I write of 'representationality') is both phallocentric and logocentric. The 'phallus' is the originary mark of difference between one thing and another (and all discourse is necessarily phallocentric, even if it were to operate in a manner that is not patriarchal). Logocentricity refers to the way in which language appears to correspond to an external reality that we can never know except through signification. In Lacan's early work, relations that appear to be only between two things, such as a thing and its mirror image, are called the 'imaginary order' and are always already structured by the symbolic. With Lacanian psychology, the only 'event' (for want of a better term) that indicts or disrupts the totalization of the symbolic order is the capitalized Real, which indicates a tear or gash in the integrity and entirety of this order. This notion, which has nothing to do with reality in the ordinary sense, is an ontological absolute, located as if 'beyond' the possibility of signification or representationality. It is impossible to imagine the Real, to integrate it within the symbolic order, to render it amenable to calculation or logic, or to attain it in any way.

Here it should be noticed that, in some of these characterizations, the Real is not entirely unlike what was described about the energetic character of the unconscious-as-repressed. However, in Lacanianism, the Real is not the voicing of subtle energies as if coming from 'outside' the symbolic order of representationality. It is merely a catastrophic rent or tear (crack or gash) within the totalization of the signifier. Like most schools of psychoanalysis, Lacanianism discards the notion of energy (thus trying to embed psychoanalysis within the euromodern masterdiscourse). Rather, the Real is associated with trauma and death—those dimensions of life that the psyche cannot assimilate and accommodate, indicating an unsurpassable fissure in the totalization of language. This then is the skimpiest synopsis of some Lacanian ideas.

It is essential for a contemporary psychoanalyst to understand Lacanianism, and to go beyond its coordinates (it may be noted that since 1984 I have published a series of criticisms of this important theoretical framework). One central problem is that the Lacanian framework does not really allow the psyche to be living as flesh, blood, and bones. For example, we can agree that the subject of the psyche—'I'—bounces along chains of signification, without being in charge of what came before or what comes after. Its pathways are governed by the upper-case 'Other' (the law and order of the symbolic system, as mentioned in Chapter One). But this begs a question: What fuels, for want of a better phrasing, the move from one signifier to the next? Yes, the law and order of signification determines what links with what, by the operations of displacement and condensation, metonym and metaphor. But this does not explain the 'life' of the movement. That is, to give an arbitrary example: Why does S_{35} give way to S_{36} then to S_{37} and so forth? Here Lacan surely might have invoked Freud's notion of psychic energy, but—as far as I have been able to tell—this is nowhere in his theoretical thinking. Instead, his elaborate notions of the subject's 'lack of being' (*manque-à-être*), which engenders desire (*désir*, as a sort of want-to-be) with its 'object-cause' (*objet (petit) a*), are theoretically introduced.

In short, Lacan is so committed to euromodern rationality, denying the possibility of subtle energies, that as early as 1955 he concocted an algebraic function, the *objet (petit) a* to designate the object-cause of a remainder that is unassimilable to signification, and thus itself unattainable. It functions theoretically as the object-cause of desire, which is like an irreducible reserve of libidinality at the centre of the 'knot' where all three orders (symbolic, imaginary, and Real) intersect. To me, it seems like a sophisticated but makeshift response to the question as to what fuels the historiciity or sequentiality of significatory chains—a convenient and expedient manoeuvre by which to deny the force of subtle energies. How much simpler and more compelling it might have been for Lacanianism to embrace Freud's notion of psychic energy—the vivacity of our fleshy, bloody, boney embodiment—the *élan vital* that lives and breathes within us and through us. However, Lacan was a child of the euromodern era, determined to render a version of 'psychoanalysis' that conforms impeccably to metaphysical assumptions about the exclusivity of rationality and logic. Although I know personally that he would have protested this conclusion, there is a sense in which Lacan's thinking describes a psyche that is more or less cadaverous.

Lacan's notion of the symbolic order emphasizes the oedipal complexities into which the subject is thrown when inducted into the symbolic order because this order conveys the primordial 'no' of the incest taboo; this theorizes the actual process of repression (Freud's *eigentliche Verdrängung*). Subsequently, Laplanche, who had trained with Lacan and later became something of a critic, elaborated Freud's notion of originary repression (*Urverdrängung*). He argues that infants are subject to the 'fundamental anthropological situation' in which their psyche is formed by the imposition of a profusion of incomprehensible messages coming—primarily—from their caretakers. As infants become positioned within the symbolic order, they retain this substratum of enigmatic messages 'repressed' within their embodiment. Laplanche seems to insist that these 'messages' are like a mélange of signifiers within us—unordered and hence active, yet interminably unintelligible. But why must these enigmatic messages be considered as signifiers? Laplanche complies with the Lacanian insistence on the assumption that everything must be understood in terms of the system of signifiers. Yet, I would argue, if Laplanche had been open to the notion of psychic energy, it would have been quite compelling to argue that infants are subjected to the imposition of energetic forces that act as enigmatic messages within the formation of their psyche. The fetishistic insistence on theorizing everything in terms of signifiers ends up limiting the value of these theoretical ideas.

Some reasons to listen to the aliveness of psychic energy

Inflamed by the prevalent euromodern ambition to expand representational knowledge, eliminate the subversive notion of psychic energies, and thus hold epistemology as having primary philosophical and clinical significance, the history of 'psychoanalysis' has almost never examined its own ontological, ethical, and metaphysical commitments. Concomitantly, without such an examination, it has licensed itself to ignore the importance of Freud's method. Yet, as Elizabeth Grosz argues in her 2017 book, whenever an epistemological enterprise stops to question itself—the conditions for its knowledge and its own lacunae or loci of nonknowledge—it is found that there is a remainder of 'issues' about being-and-becoming that fall outside of its representational systems of knowing. 'Psychoanalysis' has breezed along—or perhaps more precisely stumbled along—confident in the assumption that it comprises a progressive series of theories that permit greater knowledge about the psyche. Thus, it has had to derogate or ignore what free-associative praxis suggested to Freud; namely, that the alleged oneness of biology and psychology, so stridently asserted by neuropsychoanalysts as seamless, is actually not. Indeed, it might involve a force that subverts this material/immaterial binary. Perhaps today only a serious consideration of the power of free-associative discourse—and thence of the power of psychic energies—can rediscover Freud's discipline. Against the hegemony of the euromodern masterdiscourse, there are several reasons to counter any ambition to eliminate the rebellious notion of subtle energy.

Within the eurocentric context, there is a motley lineage of philosophy that defies the assumption that epistemology comes first, focusing instead on ontological concerns. This starts as early as the presocratic development of a vitalistic cosmology in which every element of the universe (both matter and idea) is animated by a fiery breath or 'pneuma.' It is as recent as the writings of Deleuze on the constitution of the universe as force fields—for example, the 'plane' of immanence. The latter is the unconceptualized and unconceptualizable condition of conceptuality, and the un-narratable condition of narrative (itself neither discursive nor propositional, neither intentional nor referential). Between these ancient and more recent contributions there stands much medieval philosophy as well as the 17th-century writings of Spinoza and Gottfried Leibniz, coming down to the early 19th-century Arthur Schopenhauer, who argued that all natural and human events are expressions of an insatiable *will-to-life*. Schopenhauer was significantly affected by his exposure to Asian philosophy. In turn he strongly influenced Freud and his contemporaries, Nietzsche and Henri Bergson. This is perhaps the intellectual context in which Freud, in the first two decades of his psychoanalytic labours, could assert that there must be a force coming *between* (and within) the events of matter and mind. Implied is a consideration of the character and conditions of our *being* that in a sense must precede the operations of epistemology. There follows a range of 20th-century philosophers, all of whom were influenced to some degree by psychoanalysis (Bataille, Derrida, Irigaray, and so forth). Setting aside the writings of Martin Heidegger, Deleuze is perhaps notably significant in relation to this return to ontology because he—like Levinas—insists that ethics must precede epistemology. That is, an ethic of openness to being-becoming—the opening of discourse to the movements of being-becoming—takes priority over any procedure of deciding whether the 'object' is this or that.

To sloganize what has already been argued: *If free-associative praxis is taken seriously, psychoanalysis is, foremost, an ontoethical discipline.*

Not dissimilar from the cosmology of the preSocratics, every indigenous culture of which we have record, as well as all the followers of Dharmic and Taoic spiritual traditions, believe in the operation of subtle energies, as well as the individual's capacity to have some sort of awareness of their movements. Consider here: *Umoya* from Southern African cultures (this is the Xhosa variant); *Mana* from Oceanic cultures; *Orenda* from North American cultures; *Oud* or *od* from ancient Norse and Germanic cultures, which Freud knew much about, since it was reintroduced in 1845 by Carl von Reichenbach of the Prussian Academy of Sciences; *Ruach* in Hebrew (most notably in Judaic teachings of the Kabbalah); and the Arabic notion of *Ruuh al-hayah*, which appears most notably in Sufi spiritual practices. Additionally, of course, even contemporary European cultures have become somewhat familiar with the notion of *prānā* from South Asia, and *ch'i* (*ki* or *lom*) from East and Southeast Asia.

In short, the only peoples who find the notion of subtle energies pervading the universe to be unacceptable are those under the sway of the euromodern masterdiscourse of analytico-referentiality or logical-empiricism. It is a North Atlantic derangement, enacted by the euromodern episteme that rules out the force of subtle energies and how the awareness of them influences our lived-experience.

Breaking this hold over our thinking that has been wielded by the euromodern masterdiscourse is supported not only by the lineage of philosophy that questions the metaphysical assumption of epistemology as primary but also by all the ancient wisdom traditions mentioned above. In these contexts, listening to our awareness of subtle forces that cannot be captured representationally is not to be condemned as hocus-pocus (as it has been by so many right-minded 'psychoanalysts'). Indeed, consider how we now live in an era of science that undermines the particle/wave dichotomy. Ours is the era of the uncertainty principle, of quantum interference, of gluons and quarks of different 'flavours,' tunnelling effects, nonlocality, and so forth. This is the era in which we can appreciate dynamic nonlinear complexities, and the force of action at a distance. It is an era in which the mahāyāna doctrine, which states that all events—past, present, and future—are subtly interconnected as infinite fields or lattices of energy, resonates with scientific experience.

This is not an era in which it is reasonable to dismiss the notion that the human psyche is constituted and operates within fields or planes of subtle energy that run through it and around it. The question now reverts to the ways in which—that is, ontoethical processes by which—one might cultivate an awareness of such forces.

Chapter 5

On listening free-associatively

Experiencing realities within us that are beneath and beyond our representational comprehension is a wild, and often terrifying, adventure in which our being-becoming is inevitably shaken-up and remobilized. This is precisely where the radicalized praxis of free-association takes us in a way that is profoundly healing.

Listening to unrepresentable commotions of psychic energy

The deliberate use of benign hallucinogenic materials, spontaneous eruptions of psychotic processes, certain modalities of bodywork, and deep engagement with specific practices of meditation may all be a diverse grouping of exceptions. But in the course of everyday life, only in death, orgasmic ecstasy, and traumatic eventualities are we likely to experience—in quite different ways—an awareness of realities that are not within our capacity to represent them, and never will be. Indeed, by definition, traumatic events are not uncommon occurrences that cannot be captured within our representational system. Although traumas may not occur with great frequency, everyone experiences them sooner or later. Moreover, there are normative traumas, such as separation-individuation (and the adult world's imposition of 'enigmatic messages' upon the helpless infant-toddler) and the crises of oedipality, which are inevitable in the course of each individual's acculturation. By definition, our representational capacity cannot adapt—assimilate and accommodate—to that which is traumatic.

DOI: 10.4324/9781003558262-5

Thus, such events cannot be processed or worked-through cognitively and affectively; consequently their repercussions usually remain locked within our energized embodiment.

However, a psychoanalytic session offers a contained—intimate, free, safe—timespace in which radical free-associative praxis allows us to encounter within ourselves what would otherwise be traumatic. A full-on engagement with this method permits an awareness of experiences that cannot be represented. Not to be captured within the articulations of our self-consciousness, this energetic dimension of our lived-experience comprises an exuberant and excessive force that is incessantly within and around us. In relation to this dimension, the containment of the psychoanalytic session permits patients and psychoanalysts to become adept at listening to, and sensing an awareness of, pulsations—ripples, effusions, obstructions, occlusions, and commotions—of psychic energy that run within, around, and through our psyche. With experience, the practitioner comes to listen with the 'body' as well as the 'mind.' This is, however, a very special mode of 'listening' to energies that—not being representable—cannot be held captive by interpretation.

Although not directed at the discipline of psychoanalysis, Jean-Luc Nancy's 2002 essay on listening discusses philosophically the notion of *listening-to-listen*. In a different context with quite divergent meaning, Haydée Faimberg introduced the same term to psychoanalysis in 1981, subsequently elaborating it in relation to *Nachträglichkeit*. What these different usages have in common is the advocacy of a decentred mode of listening—an absenting of, or holding-in-abeyance, the epistemological subject who is determined to make sense of 'what's what.' Nancy elaborates the notion by contrasting it with hearing or 'listening-to-hear.' The latter involves the techniques of listening-in-order-to-understand, listening-to-interpret—aiming to arrive at the possibility of re-presenting. That is, aiming to arrive at interpretation and insight.

If it is not to devolve into a theory-driven psychotherapeutic procedure, it is imperative in psycho-*analysis* that both the psychoanalyst's and the patient's listening not be reduced to hearing. In Nancy's essay, the strongest example of listening-to-listen is the appreciation of music. That is, listening and appreciating without knowledge or any determination to know, in the sense of represent. Here one might both whimsically and seriously consider Dany Nobus and Malcolm Quinn's 2005 Lacanian recommendation to psychoanalysts: 'Know nothing, stay stupid.' Less aphoristically, Scarfone has also discussed how believing that one knows readily obstructs the processes of listening to what *is*. There is surely a sense in which, when exposed to a musical piece, the more one strains to interpret it the less one is actually listening to it. The more one's motive to hear it is to be able to play it again—to *re*present it—the less one is actually appreciating it by listening to it in its present immediacy. Thus, having the expertise of a professional musicologist—the same as having knowledge of the theories of 'psychoanalysis'—actually impedes and detracts from one's capacity for listening-to-listen.

As opposed to hearing, this mode of listening is more like allowing oneself to *resonate* to the music, by foregoing the effort to understand it (and relinquishing the determination to repeat or represent it). Resonating is more like our response to the erotic embrace of a lover (even if this response is discordantly toned). Here one might think of Nancy's various writings on touch, nudity, skin, and the body (for example, his 1992 *Corpus*, which was celebrated in Derrida's *On Touching*), and also of Irigaray's philosophy of the caress.

In listening-to-listen, one enjoys an awareness of something like what Eugene Gendlin and others such as Michael Eigen call a *felt-sense*. This is not an intuition, which is, by definition, a future-oriented image or representation. Rather, it is the immediacy of an inner awareness that can perhaps be uttered, but not in an articulate manner, and that does not drive towards some future (mis) representation. Even when the process is painful, to listen-to-listen is to allow oneself to be touched by whatever is uttered in the movement of radicalized free-association—as if by a lover. The meaningfulness of such a caressive flow defies interpretation.

Free-associative listening is a prime example of listening-to-listen as an erotically embodied praxis, in which the method's receptivity—to the voicing of what is otherwise than representationality—necessarily involves a rigorous demissioning, renunciation, or deconstruction of the functions and the demands of making sense. It does not expand the repertoire of reflective self-consciousness but rather accrues to our awareness of the flow and flux of what *is*—the momentum of our being-becoming. With this in focus, we can now turn to consider the workplay of the patient and that of the psychoanalyst in the course of each psycho-*analytic* session.

Notes on being a patient in psychoanalysis

Individuals who imagine that they need and wish to enter into psychoanalysis must wait for the right practitioner to appear. Sadly, for many, this never happens. A qualified psychoanalyst is necessary for three reasons.

First, if it is to become genuinely psycho-*analytic*, the process is far too unsettling, disturbing, and even terrifying to engage without having the secure knowledge that one has a 'friend,' whose immediate *presence* is felt even in silence. Note here how Pythagoras defined a friend as one who accompanies you on a journey, facilitating your perseverance on the road to a happier life.

Second, even as a silent interlocutor, the psychoanalyst is necessary as the 'friend' who sets the frame of the treatment. That is, the practitioner explains the usefulness of the couch, excludes all third-parties (including consultants, presentations at seminars, and note-taking even if only intended for private future use), begins and ends each sessional hour with utmost punctuality, insists on prompt payment of a reasonable fee, and tenderly declines the patient's longings for physical connection. The psychoanalyst thus facilitates the establishment of a relationship founded on the blessings of a unique degree of intimacy, freedom, and safety. Patients could not possibly engage in the chaotic and regressive processes of radical free-association if they did not have the security of knowing that these factors were assured. For example, patients could not allow themselves to 'regress' into radical free-association, which is an altered condition of consciousness, unless they know that, at the end of the session, they are going to have to get off the couch and proceed with their quotidian lives. Patients cannot fully engage their feelings for the psychoanalyst—nor can they internalize the benefits of a relationship that performatively disconfirms historical patterns—if they are beholden to this practitioner. Thus it is necessary that there be a transactional reciprocity, and that patients know that they are taking care of their psychoanalyst by paying her/him a reasonable portion of her/his living expenses. And so on—without this 'frame' there can be no psychoanalysis.

Third, one cannot free-associate radically except in the presence of a qualified psychoanalyst. Since one's own stream of consciousness is private, it may seem counterintuitive to suggest that one cannot utter it aloud unless this silent interlocutor is present. However, that legendary individual—the American 'psychoanalyst' who talked into a recording device for a daily 50-minute 'session' and then listened 'analytically' to his own ramblings—launched a misleading and pernicious myth in claiming that he was engaged in a productive self-analysis. Whereas this man may have been doing some useful psychotherapy on himself (or he may not, but rather he might be leading himself into more complex modes of self-mystification), he cannot possibly have been doing psycho-*analysis* at all. You can do the experiment for yourself: Close your eyes and attempt to speak out loud your 'stream of consciousness' as close as you are able (if you find yourself needing to feel that someone is listening, you can even address your babbling remarks to your 'god'). You will certainly find that, before too long, you will either fall silent or lapse into narrative recitation. You will not be free-associating (even in the soft mode of this method). Even if you perform this exercise in the presence of a friend who is not a psychoanalyst, you will fail after a brief beginning. In short, a qualified psychoanalyst, who is present with you, thoroughly alive, and adept at listening-to-listen to a patient's utterances, is essential for this complex process to ensue.

The presence of a relatively silent listener is required not only for the reasons just mentioned but also, if the discourse is to become psycho-*analytic*, to function for the patient both as a specific lower-case *other* and as emblematic of the upper-case *Other* (the distinctions introduced in Chapter One). This is what an authentic training in psychoanalysis enables an individual to accomplish. As the patient's 'friend' and healer, the psychoanalyst is the 'other' who—compassionately, appreciatively, and graciously—addresses each of the patient's multifarious resistances to free-association, which will repeatedly arise almost continuously.

This other person in the session is not there to generate interpretations of latent themes, as does a psychotherapist, but only to address resistances. As these occur, the psychoanalyst must intervene to facilitate the patient's readiness to relinquish such aversions to the processes of free-associative expression, allowing their obstructiveness to dissolve. Yet additionally, in refusing to be either an ordinary conversationalist or a mundane authority on what's what—that is, by remaining nonresponsively silent and refraining from substantive interpretation—the psychoanalyst's presence emblematizes the position of the Other, as the deathful void into which we all speak, whether or not we are aware of it. It is the realization of this void that makes the discourse of psycho-*analysis* not only unsettling but potentially terrifying, even while it is profoundly healing.

Although the right practitioner may have appeared and the frame of treatment be available, patients cannot simply jump into a work-playing relationship with their psychoanalyst and immediately immerse themselves in a full-on psychoanalytic process. I invite you to reconsider the fictitious conversation with your fabled Great Aunt, who was dramatically featured in Chapter Two. As comfortable as you might have felt in the course of the somewhat psychotherapeutic moments you shared with her, you would not have wanted to blurt out every thought, feeling, or image that came into your mind as the two of you chatted together. For the same reason, as has been noted, there is an initial phase of the psychoanalytic relationship that typically lasts about a year before a truly psychoanalytic process gets underway. This is a somewhat psychotherapeutic phase in that the patient and psychoanalyst have to have some understanding of what's what before they can relinquish the need to understand. Then they have to become ready to abandon judgmentalism and have their interpretations dismantled or deconstructed (for judgment inheres to all interpretation). It is as if some procedures of hearing each other—accumulating the concrete experiences of intimacy, freedom, and safety that build a psychoanalytic alliance—are required before the psychoanalytic duo can move towards a mutual process of listening-to-listen that proceeds beyond representational understanding.

One cannot underestimate how intrepid the patient must be in proceeding from doing a psychotherapeutic procedure to experiencing the psycho-*analytic* process. Psychotherapy can be very unsettling when familiar perceptions, attitudes, and convictions are called into question, and as familiar patterns of relating are exposed when reenacted with the practitioner as 'transference.' In psychotherapy, the patient's inner theatre of representations is explored, and much will be subjected to reinterpretation. Anxiety, guilt, shame, and periods of rageful disorganization as well as erotic longing are all likely to arise in various ways, and more often than not the psychotherapeutic patient goes through periods of great personal difficulty precipitated by the procedure. However, if and when a psychotherapeutic procedure moves into a psycho-*analytic* process (for example, after a successful initial phase of the workplay), the patient can find the treatment both more erotically enjoyable and yet far more forbiddingly frightening (than it was in psychotherapy). The process can be depicted in the following manner.

The patient is physically comfortable, lying on the couch. The horizontality permits awareness of bodily sensations, as well as fluxes in the shifting of embodied psychic energy (in a different way than does the verticality of the psychoanalyst). The patient's eyes are preferably kept shut for the duration of the session because this minimizes her/his distraction from external stimuli and hence facilitates awareness of internal sensations. Although there may well be times in which patients experience rage and hatred towards the psychoanalyst, in general they simply feel the presence of a compassionate friend seated out of sight. This is a presence in which this friend is well able to hear every utterance the patient makes, to see every shift in the patient's bodily expressions, and even to smell the patient's odours. The patient is invited to speak free-associatively, to express without censorship and to listen. Invariably, the patient begins with the soft or story-telling mode of speaking. Even this can be quite disturbing, often causing the patient to realize that they are more troubled than they initially anticipated. However, as the patient's free-associative expression becomes more radical—implying the crucial shift from psychotherapeutic procedure to psychoanalytic process—it can be anticipated that resistances will intensify.

Resistances to free-association are always abundant, from the beginning to the end of a psychoanalytic treatment (and we will shortly discuss their character). A skilful practitioner addresses these phenomena non-combatively (which is not always the way that Freud described how they should be addressed). That is, in a manner that explicitly appreciates the importance of resistances for the patient's sense of inner well-being (from the standpoint of the patient's current psychic reality), and that thereby allows the patient willingly to relinquish these obstructions, as if letting them spontaneously dissolve. Only under this sort of tender and considerate disposition can patients gradually move from soft free-association to a radicalized mode of this praxis.

As already suggested, this move from a psychotherapeutic procedure into a psychoanalytic process is erotically pleasant and potentially terrifying. It can seem to the patient as if they are cast adrift in a vast ocean of chaotic felt-senses, deprived of the familiar coordinates of self and world. This is the psycho-*analytic* process that involves a breaking-down of, or detachment from, representational law and order. As the repressive functions of representation (insight, interpretation, understanding) are subverted, the patient becomes more able to listen to the disruptive felt-senses of repressed forces. This listening-to-listen becomes a maieutics of the repressed—an unsaying or subversion of interpretation that allows repressed energies a more exposed and strident voicing within us. A non-representational awareness of the repressed is thus cultivated. The enunciations of psychic energies are uttered not only through words, nor even exclusively in sounds—somatic phenomena are equally embraced. All such expressions arise from a free-associative surrender to the commotions of psychic energy. This is the voicing of the repressed, the awareness of which heals us—despite that it can never be translated into our representational comprehension. For both patient and psychoanalyst, the process is a wild ride.

Notes on doing psychoanalysis as a practitioner

Being a psychoanalyst is not a job, nor merely a profession. Rather, it is a calling. As such, it permeates the entire life of the practitioner (and has nothing to do with holding a diploma from an established training institute). Once one has genuinely become a psychoanalyst, one never stops being a psychoanalyst.

Nevertheless, there are distinctive tasks, roles, and attitudinal positions that psychoanalysts must perform when in session with a patient, and these all pertain to the way in which they enable and empower the practitioner to listen to the patient free-associatively. It is true that sometimes, for the psychoanalyst who has acquired the art of listening-to-listen, it can become challenging to revert to paying attention to the ordinary meaningfulness of the speech-acts and language-games of ordinary discourse. This challenge requires an internal activity of parsing and partitioning that has to be acquired in the course of the individual's formation as a psychoanalyst. Within the session—the 'clinic' as Lacanians would call it—the psychoanalyst has a threefold task, as has already been indicated.

First, s/he must establish and maintain, with an exemplary single-mindedness, the frame of the treatment and, by this means, build a psychoanalytic alliance with the patient; the practitioner befriends the patient.

Second the psychoanalyst must address resistances to facilitate the patient's move away from the psychotherapeutic demand for interpretations and elaborated narratives that inevitably occupy a major portion of the initial phase of the treatment. This entails the patient's move from soft free-association towards a progressively more full-on engagement with this method. This entails diverse approaches by which to address the patient's anxieties, fears, and moments of disequilibrium. Thus the psychoanalyst's contribution initially addresses the patient's resistance even to the soft or story-telling mode of free-association—for example, the patient insists on having an agenda or on completing her/his particular narrations, and in various ways s/he declines to utter spontaneously whatever 'comes to mind' or 'comes to body.' In these ways, the patient might seem to be complying with the invitation to free-associate but is still clinging to the notion that all things must eventually make sense. Next comes a step at which many practitioners falter. For psycho-*analysis* to occur, the psychoanalyst must gradually move towards addressing the resistances of patients who comply with the soft mode of free-associative narrating but resist—often strenuously—expressing themselves in the more radical mode, which is narratologically transgressive. It is invariably found that the resistances to story-telling free-associatively may be powerful but are far less so than the resistances to radicalized free-association. This is largely because the latter, violating the narratological imperative, may include incomprehensible wording, noises, and somatic phenomena. In short, contrasted with a psychotherapeutic procedure, the utterances of a psychoanalytic process break—often dramatically—with the law and order of making sense, and thus are more challenging to share out loud as the process casts the patient into the turbulence of de-repressed energies.

The address of the patient's resistances must never be combative or critical, for their role in maintaining the patient's sense of well-being must always be explicitly appreciated. This dimension of the psychoanalyst's contribution—as serious and crucial as the task is—does not necessarily have to be undertaken in a weighty constative manner. When patients and practitioners are in the right sort of 'working alliance,' playfulness may be powerfully effective in freeing the former to relinquish their resistances. I have personally found that all sorts of noises (e.g., grunt, sigh, or ahem), ironic exclamations (e.g., oh no!, ouch, or again?), and even expletives (e.g., shit!) may facilitate patients' becoming amused by their own resisting. After all, irony and a licence to be outrageous are among the psychoanalyst's strongest attributes. On occasion, I will, if called for, burst into song. Of course, resistances are always being taken seriously by the practitioner, and sometimes—for example, when the patient becomes physically threatening or undresses seductively—the best way to address resistances is to remain silent, be utterly calm, and move one's breathing deeply into the abdomen. In all these examples, the way in which resistances are addressed by the psychoanalyst recognizes appreciatively that these interferences or obstructions to the flow of free-associative expression are—from the standpoint of the patient's psychic reality—vitally important for her/his equilibrium and well-being. Only if resistances are addressed in this manner that acknowledges their importance to the patient's inner world—that is, compassionately, appreciatively, and graciously—can the patient ever feel safe to relinquish them and deepen her/his commitment to free-associative expression.

The third task of the psychoanalyst pivots not on her/his activity in addressing resistances to radicalized free-associative praxis, but rather on positioning as present but in nonresponsive silence an absenting presence. No longer an 'other' with whom the patient might engage in speech-acts and language-games, the psychoanalyst becomes emblematic of the Other, an absenting presence, which is—in relation to the representationality of what we call our 'mind'—the deathful void into which we all express ourselves.

Here we come again to my post-Lacanian riff on the notion of the psychoanalyst as emblematizing the upper-case Other. To appreciate psycho-*analysis* as such, it is vitally important not only to grasp appreciatively the basics of Lacanianism (as we initiated in Chapter Four) but also to dissent strenuously from the practices of the Lacanian 'clinic.' The clinical brilliance of Lacan's notion is the recognition that the patient's demand that the psychoanalyst be the 'one who knows,' the *sujet suppose savoir*, must be thwarted. Ultimately, psycho-*analysis* is a process of deconstructing understandings and surrendering to the aliveness of not-understanding (un-understanding, *unverständnis*, was Freud's term, although this condition does *not* imply any lack of awareness).

In Lacan's philosophical terminology, the psychoanalyst poses as, and the patient takes the psychoanalyst as, the Other, although in 'reality' the former knows nothing. The psychoanalyst as Other is positioned as if the Dead Father, who mythically birthed the Symbolic Order (this 'order' is more or less how I am using the term 'representationality'). However, in Lacanian theorizing, the Other is the empty position—as if the anchoring centrepoint—of the phallus that is the source of all possible signification. Yet with Lacanianism, there is no opening for an *otherwise* mode of meaningfulness, a mode that eludes the totality of the pathways of the signifier and cannot be captured within the permutations and combinations of displacement and condensation. Indeed there is the (non)register of the 'Real' that intimates the limits of signification, but the notion of this catastrophic rent or tear is never allowed flesh, blood and bones (as discussed in the previous chapter).

The Lacanian practitioner is positioned as the Other so that indeed the patient can realize the void into which her/his expressions are directed. However, beyond this tenet, the Lacanian 'clinic' can become a disaster. The practitioner emblematizes a notion of the Other that does not even have to be present. Indeed, it is notorious how Lacan himself could foreshorten sessions to a few minutes, leave the consulting room to do an errand while the patient was speaking, and fall asleep (with the patient still being charged a full fee). Such chicanery is theoretically justifiable—perhaps, with a substantial ingredient of sophistry—*if* one insists that the psychoanalyst in the position of the Other is nothing but an absolute absence. But this is profoundly mistaken—depending upon Lacan's determination to rule out the notion of psycho-*analysis* as an energetic praxis. Lacanianism must be saluted as the most important theorizing since Freud, for it is the apotheosis of efforts to make 'psychoanalysis' conform to the precepts of the euromodern masterdiscourse. But accordingly, it is the downfall of the discipline.

The psychoanalyst addresses the patient's resistances and does indeed position her/himself in nonresponsive silence, as if outside the domain of representationality. But this is a position of *otherwiseness* (rather than abstraction of the 'Other'). In being an absenting presence, the psychoanalyst emblematizes the deathfulness of all being-becoming—this is not an absolute void but the aliveness of a chaos of unrepresentable, but meaningful, energies. The psychoanalyst receives the psychic energies of the patient, and vice versa. This is an un-understandable process, essential to which is free-associative listening-to-listen. To appreciate this further, we must turn to the psychoanalytic attitude and the way in which it uniquely facilitates listening-to-listen—that is, listening free-associatively to the embodied movement of psychic energies, the force of the repressed, which is within but beyond the comprehension of representability.

The psychoanalyst's attitude

It can be inferred from what has been presented that as they engage deeply in radicalized free-associative praxis patients in psychoanalysis are effectively in an altered condition of consciousness. This might be described as a heightened acuity of awareness, especially of embodied movements of energy (and the intimations of emotion), and concomitantly a decreased commitment to representational making-sense (and the augmentation of self-consciousness, as the realm of 'I-Now-Is'). So too is the psychoanalyst in an altered state. It is quite unlike the alterations induced by cathartic discharge, by hypnosis (which is famously the precursor of Freud's discovery), or by the judicious use of hallucinogenic plant medicine. It is different in that, even after a mere 50-minute session, the patient emerges better able to integrate the experience, living a little more freely in terms of our human repetition-compulsivity. The effects of psychoanalysis are singularly long-lasting and often subtle.

Much has been written recently about the state of mind of the psychoanalyst—one thinks here of Fred Busch's 2019 summary on contemporary thinking about the psychoanalyst's 'reveries' and the impact of Wilfred Bion's important contributions. However, the developments in method that Busch discusses have continued to be imbued with the prioritization of epistemology—that is, the psychoanalyst's 'state of mind' is mostly of concern in that it must be usefully directed towards interpretation of the patient's 'mind.' Nevertheless, the way practitioners open themselves to trance-like phenomena that are inspired by the presence of the patient—like waking dreams and waking nightmares—is crucial to the challenge of listening to the patient free-associatively.

It is only in the initial phase of treatment that psychoanalysts should be at all preoccupied with 'figuring things out' on behalf of the patient. In all other moments, psychoanalysts have to learn the art of listening-to-listen, which requires that they be in something of a trance (and not trying to hear too much). This is what, I believe, Freud was trying to describe with his notion of evenly-weaving attention (*gleichswebende Aufmerksamkeit*). 'Attention' may be a less than optimal term because it often connotes a state of concentration (although it is true that the psychoanalyst must be 'attending,' in the sense of being present; moreover, at least in my imagination, the common translation of *gleichswebende* as 'hovering' is thoroughly misleading as it suggests busy fluttering of a foraging bee ready to strike upon the nearest cache of pollen). Contrary to such a 'hunting and gathering' attitude, whether of mutual benefit or not, surely the more refined point of *gleichswebende Aufmerksamkeit* is that the patient is the psychoanalyst's muse—amusedly so—and the latter's mostly silent musing opens the patient's discourse to a deeper and more intense praxis of free-association. The psychoanalyst comes under the spell of the patient, listening with an intensified acuity of awareness in relation to movements of energy within her/himself and between her/himself and the patient. In a state close to hypnagogia, psychoanalysts methodically relinquish the stringencies of rational thinking—operating in a nearly unmitigated state of cogitative or ratiocinative stupor, in which whatever they think they might know is undone or deconstructed. This is opening oneself to the awareness of psychic energies; it is listening *otherwise*.

None of these aspects of the psychoanalyst's workplay with the patient would be possible without the practitioner maintaining what can be called the psychoanalytic 'attitude.' It is necessary for the free-associative praxis of listening-to-listen and has three aspects—aspects that may initially seem paradoxical in relation to each other but are essentially inwoven.

First, the psychoanalyst must be a passionately engaged *presence* for the patient. At all times the patient needs a felt sense of the psychoanalyst sitting quietly out of sight. With those patients who are inclined to retreat into themselves, it may be necessary for the practitioner occasionally to shift in the chair or do something similar so that the patient's sense of connection is maintained. Equally, while psychoanalysts listen to their own inner images and sensations, they are careful not to leave the session in their mind—to lose their connection with the patient and go into 'their own material.' Examples of retreating practitioners would be those who are busy contemplating the menu for dinner, or imagining their next summer vacation—although often, even these 'departures' from the discourse of the session may be obscurely prompted by the patient's material.

In this commitment to being present with the patient, the passionate engagement of the psychoanalyst is neither an issue of being sympathetic nor of being empathetic. Rather it is a matter of compassion and enjoyment. Compassion entails a deep awareness of the patient's suffering and a wish to facilitate a process whereby patients might free themselves from their imprisonment in repetition-compulsivity. The psychoanalyst's enjoyment of their patients, even while they are suffering and even when they may be viciously hateful and ugly towards the psychoanalysis, is a spiritual praxis of 'finding the joy in'—that is, being steadfastly aware of an exultancy in the liveliness of life that girds even the most tragic of circumstances.

Second, the psychoanalyst must be *equanimous* in all circumstances. This implies that even while practitioners may well (and indeed should) have intense feelings for and with the patient they do not get thrown by them, do not enact them, and do not allow them to interfere with the continuity of the psychoanalytic process. The maintenance of equanimity is mostly achieved by the psychoanalyst remaining in the awareness of her/his breathing and, when finding her/himself aroused, moving the breath down into the abdomen.

The third necessary quality of the psychoanalytic 'attitude' is *neutrality*, which implies a radical stance of non-judgmentalism. This is perhaps the most challenging dimension of training as an individual progresses from being a psychotherapist towards being authentically a psychoanalyst. The trainee has to be incessantly reminded that s/he does *not* know better than the patient how the patient's life should be conducted. To give an extreme example, the practitioner cannot decide that patients should not suicide (although in practice clinicians do have a communal responsibility to deter patients from damaging or ending the lives of others). There are no 'shoulds' or 'should-nots' in psychoanalysis; the discrimination between the 'good' and the 'bad' is not up to the psychoanalyst.

More generally, relinquishing all judgmentalism is part and parcel of the requirement that interpretations and theories must all be deconstructed and any attachment to them set aside, held in abeyance, or bracketed-off. It should be very clear by now that the epistemology that treats the patient's functioning as 'object' (for the practitioner, or for the patient, as epistemological 'subject') may be integral to coaching or counselling, and may be somewhat necessary in psychotherapy, but it has no place in psycho-*analysis*. To engage in a psychoanalytic process is to abrogate any attachment to diagnosis, formulation, interpretation, and insight. Rather, it is to learn to listen—listening-to-listen—to the flux and flow of what *is*, the being-becoming of the patient and of the psychoanalyst.

To serve the being-becoming of the patient, the psychoanalyst thus has to be profoundly ethical but utterly amoral. S/he sets aside all judgment as to whether what the patient is saying and doing amounts to something 'good' or something 'bad.' Yet s/he is radically ethical in being committed to opening discourse to whatever *is*. This implies listening to whatever *is* in the dimension of being-becoming, not in order to judge it, but rather to bring it into the light—opening our being-becoming to express itself not only to that which is 'other' than the representations of self-consciousness that we know but also to that which is *otherwise* than representationality, the repressed within us. This ethicality—the ontoethicality—of opening to whatever *is* requires that we listen as much, or more, to the 'body' as to the 'mind.'

Listening free-associatively to our erotic embodiment

The repressed and the de-repressive motions of psychic energy that course within our bodymind, as well as the articulations and de-articulations of cosmic energies that vibrate through us and around us, are never subject to being *heard* (although they can be listened to, with awareness). They cannot be captured by the manoeuvres of our ratiocinative—rational—thinking. All the permutations and combinations—the condensations and displacements—of representationality inevitably miss the voicing of this force within us, since it is otherwise than that which can be represented. As has been discussed, the traces of repression fail to be translated back into representation and are thus forever unavailable to our reflective self-consciousness. They elude captivation even though they disrupt the coherence, cogency, and continuity of our self-conscious capacity to represent ourselves and our worlds. In relation to the representations through which psychic energy pulses, the meaningfulness of this force always remains an exuberant and enigmatic excess. Although it cannot be articulated in our reflectively representational self-consciousness (as 'I-Now-Is'), we can become aware of it as a felt-sense of movement within us. Listening-to-listen is a vivacious process of listening through and with our erotic embodiment—this is entailed by the radicality of free-associative praxis.

The patient and the psychoanalyst commune in a field of psychic energy that permeates their erotic embodiments. As noted, they may share understandings—thoughts and feelings—in words or other modes of discourse, but the energies that pass through and between them comprise an excessive exuberance of elusive meaningfulness, a spatiotemporal kinesis of presence that cannot be captured in *re*-presentation. A praxis that invites the being-becoming of our erotic embodiment—the vivacity of our bodymind—to express itself must not only dismantle the power of the representational constructions that govern us, obstructing our capacity for awareness, but also must listen with awareness to the waves of psychic energy within us. This is what radicalized free-association offers us, and it necessarily turns our 'evenly-weaving attention' inwards towards the kinesis of erotic embodiment—the psychoanalyst's becomes attuned to the patient's.

As Freud discovered—although never put across in quite this phrasing—psychic energy ebbs and flows within us. In every moment of instantiated meaning, there are simultaneous shifts *both* in which psychic energy drains away from a somatic or cognitive formation, which is the deathfulness of life itself (*Todestrieb), and* in which such energy invests (*Besetzung*) itself in such formations, which is the liveliness of life itself (*Lebenstrieb*). It is only by free-associative listening-to-listen with the entirety of our bodymind that we can unlock the pervasive formations of repetition-compulsivity that imprison us.

Of course, there is a lopsidedness to the psychoanalytic relationship. The relaxed horizontality of patients on the couch, combined with their almost total control over the discursive initiatives of the session, places their physicality in a sort of anti-narrational laterality that subverts the institutionalized conventions of conversational making-sense (this is not entirely unlike Guattari's notion of 'transversality'). By contrast, the comfortable verticality of psychoanalysts better enables them to address their own resistances to the free-associative flow while also attending to those of the patient. In a relaxed manner, both positions facilitate the processes of 'listening with the body,' albeit with somewhat different emphases on the addressing of resistances.

The requirement that the psychoanalyst (and eventually the patient) must listen as much, or more, to the 'body' as to the 'mind' is challenging. This is because it can induce a dizzying sense of dislocation or even depersonalization that the practitioner has to regulate internally. If it were just a task of listening, on one's own, to the flow of energies that comes to us from without and from within the bodymind (the deathfulness and lifefulness of the incessant kinesis of psychic energy), then the way that permits this listening-to-listen with least hindrances is to engage the process while moving the body. That is, listening-to-listen and becoming aware of the kinesis within and without while dancing improvisationally and spontaneously—in a way that relinquishes both the demands of choreography and the feelings or fantasies that one so often has about 'what one looks like.' But of course this is not to be done in the treatment framework within which the patient and the psychoanalyst encounter each other's energies—simply because dancing together cannot but touch too closely on an—inescapably incestuous—erotic enactment.

For psychoanalysts to fully engage in listening-to-listen free-associatively to the messaging of both their own erotic embodiment and the patient's is daunting—not least because the psychoanalyst's own sense of self and world is perpetually thrown into question. Elsewhere I have suggested that the main reason that some psychoanalytic treatments can be 'unsuccessful'—which really means that the psychoanalyst and the patient fail to get into a psychoanalytic process—stems from the practitioner's narcissism. That is, the egotistic investment that 'psychoanalysts' have in securing their sense of self. In a somewhat but not entirely different vein, Lacan suggested that the prime resistances to psychoanalysis are those of the psychoanalyst. Interestingly, what he proposes, as early as the *Séminaires* of 1954 and 1955, is that 'there is only one resistance' to psychoanalysis and that is of the 'psychoanalyst' who thinks it is his (*sic*) job to interpret for the patient the patient's desires—that is, the practitioner who is actually doing some sort of psychotherapy.

We can conclude that a central factor in the discipline's history (in which 'psychoanalysis' has devolved into the procedures of psychotherapy), and the major factor in all the disdainful misunderstanding of Freud's revolutionary method, is that the praxis of free-associating and of listening free-associatively, despite its unique healing properties, is inordinately difficult.

Concluding note

Liberatory truthfulness!

Psychoanalysis needs to be rediscovered. It now has a long history of being identified as a jumbled set of theories about mental functioning, as techniques for knowing the designated patient in terms of such a theory, and thus as a disjointed family of psychotherapeutic endeavours. It urgently needs to be divorced from these mistaken standpoints in order for its discipline to be fully and properly appreciated as the process of healing by free-associative praxis. That is a challenge of reclamation to which this essay contributes.

Although the Lacanian clinic is something of an exception (in that its aim is not therapeutic in the ordinary sense), the various theories and techniques of contemporary 'psychoanalysis' all conceive of a successful course of psychotherapy as a procedure that helps the patient to arrive at a 'better' system of thoughts, feelings, wishes, and fantasies about the self and its world—a system by which the patient's conduct comes to be governed more adaptively. The system may now be 'better'—with heartfelt, yet somewhat acerbic, gratitude to both the psychotherapist and the psychotherapeutic enterprise. Regrettably, the organization of this system of representations is still under the sway of repetition-compulsivity, even if it seems like a 'successful' trade. That is, what is now to be repeated is more 'adaptive' than whatever it replaced but is ruled by repetition nonetheless. For example, the formulation of an uncomfortable insight is 'better' than the construction of the annoying symptom, although both retain an analogous temporal structure of governance. Overtly or covertly, psychotherapeutic techniques are underpinned by the

DOI: 10.4324/9781003558262-6

prioritization of knowing and of coming to 'know better.' They trade in interpretations, operating within the possibilities of representational transformation. Epistemological issues—along with moralizing conventionalities—come first. This is *not* the psychoanalysis that needs to be rediscovered.

If change is desirable, then the central issue of clinical concern should be the bodymind's contrivances that deter spontaneity—the automatic mechanisms or mandated stratagems that, in the interest of defending the psyche, actually reproduce and perpetuate suffering that might otherwise be relinquished. These 'defences'—inner blockages and circuitries of psychic energy, as well as inhibitions and obstacles in both reflectivity and awareness—are almost always buttressed by sociocultural conventions. They are supposed to protect us from pain—yet there is no spontaneity and no liberation from suffering without a journey that is painful. 'Defences' can thus become an impediment to the re-mobilized freeing of energies and our potential for joy in the liveliness of life itself. In this context, one might imagine that every 'psychoanalyst' would both centralize the notion of the repetition-compulsion in their clinical interventions and be outspoken critics of oppressive sociocultural arrangements. But this is not so.

One might excuse those clinicians, who understand almost everything in terms of deficit and deficiency—and whose practice might be described as a matter of plastering over the cracks in a wall that is already wobbling under the strain of its own weightiness—and who thence serve as angels of compensatory care. However, in no sense is this a practice of curing the ailment. Rather, it is the palliative medicine of acculturation, to which Freud's project never seems to have set out to contribute. If one reviews all the available information about Freud's contact with patients (not just the case histories he reported), one is impressed by his commitment to relieve unnecessary suffering. But such a challenge is never without pain, and nowhere does one get the impression that his goal is to have the patient blend with convention—this is particularly noticeable in what we know about his clinical contacts, both formal and informal, with writers and artists. There is little in Freud's writings that seriously suggests that he is committed to telling patients that they should be this way rather than that. Psychoanalytic processes are determinedly amoral.

As one of the triumvirate of the 'school of suspicion' along with Marx and Nietzsche, Freud—at least in the initiation of his discipline and despite being a very serious 'man of science'—was something of a rebel, a dissident out to unmask and demystify. That is, to deconstruct processively, or to interrogate in a negatively dialectical movement, those sociocultural conventions that constitute the tyranny of normativity and thus reinforce our psychic imprisonment in repetition-compulsivity. He was some sort of revolutionary, as indeed those who are genuine psychoanalysts still are in today's world—a world that is overwhelmed with depression and anxiety, as well as being on the brink of destruction.

At least in the first two decades of psychoanalysis the 'man of science' knew himself to be an unruly dissident. For example, in Freud's day and age, whenever bourgeois ladies went picnicking in the Viennese woods and needed to urinate or defecate, the unspoken convention was that they should tell the assembled company that they were 'going for a walk to pick wildflowers' and thus they secured their privacy. In his 1910 paper on the future prospects of his discipline, Freud implies that the psychoanalyst is somewhat like a troublemaker (*Boshafter*), who attends this picnic in order to distribute flyers that read 'Ladies, if you want to piss or shit just announce that you are going for a walk to pick wildflowers.' This confrontive way of addressing the communal resistance to honesty and candour—the collective refusal to be open to what *is* actually happening—disrupts this piece of the sociocultural system. This is one model for the psychoanalyst-as-rebel, but it does not go far enough.

The precept that our psychic life is under the governance of repetition-compulsivity should surely be central to any healing discipline. However, if we turn to the major theoretical lineages of 'psychoanalysis'—ego-psychological, object-relational, self-psychological, and relational or interpersonal therapies—as well as to the Lacanian clinic, one finds that we lack strikingly convincing explanations as to why humans reproduce their own suffering. As formulated in these various theories, our understanding of the compulsion to repeat is only a tad more sophisticated than your Great Aunt's aphorism that 'people usually continue to do what they have always continued to do.' In short, despite all the theorizing that has been promulgated since the second decade of the 20th century, the question why the repetition-compulsion governs our psychic life so powerfully and so pervasively—why we persist in compulsively repeating thoughts, feelings, wishes, fantasies, and actions that do not serve us—remains quite enigmatic. This rather extraordinary enigma is connected to unresolved questions as to why humans have irreparably trashed their own habitat, why we seem incapable of refraining from violent conflict, oppression and exploitation, as well as why our species is uniquely suicidal.

The repetition-compulsion is an empirical fact that is more or less theoretically unexplained—or at the very least insufficiently explained. It bears profoundly on contradictorious interactions between the subject of self-consciousness (the contentless 'I-Now-Is' of all reflectivity) and the effects of forces both suppressed and repressed.

Nowhere in this essay am I suggesting that a superior account of the repetition-compulsion is being provided. Rather what has been argued is that free-association is praxis, the priority of which is not to interpret self and world further but to change them by subverting the enclosures of interpretation. Ultimately, the method is not engaged in order to generate new theory. The central thesis of this essay is that free-association, when engaged full-on, comprises a uniquely and radically effective method by which the psychoanalyst and the patient collaborate to conduct—what might be depicted as—nonviolent guerilla warfare against repetition-compulsivity.

With the exception of the Lacanian clinic, which has already been criticized for avoiding the power of psychic energy (as well as the resources of flesh, blood, and bones), none of the techniques derived from the theories of 'psychoanalysis' listed above can achieve any sort of freeing from the repetition-compulsion's governance over our bodymind's functioning. This is precisely because they operate entirely within the domain of that which is represented or can potentially be represented—that which can, sooner or later, be *re*-presentationally understood in the realm of the 'I-Now-Is.' They trade in interpretations aimed at the amplification of representational self-consciousness through the reflective internalization (assimilation and accommodation) of 'new' interpretative understandings. By contrast, expressing and listening in a way that is radically free-associative propels the subject beneath and beyond the realm of the representable. It opens us to an awareness of that which cannot be represented—the movement of psychic energies within and around us.

To summarize this: Whereas psychotherapeutic procedures are representationally transformative, the processes of psychoanalysis are a uniquely transmutative way of listening with awareness to the energetic subtleties of our being-becoming. The discipline has been mistakenly characterized merely as a practice of interpretation that amplifies the scope of our self-consciousness. It is to be hoped that the investigation of free-association sketched in this essay conclusively demonstrates the egregious error of this characterization. The mistake is maintained by the refusal to be open to the notion that the human condition is composed of more than matter and mind. That is, the construction and elaboration of 'psychoanalytic' theories—from the ego-psychological to the Lacanian—has been constricted, delimited, and distorted by conformity to the euromodern masterdiscourse. The latter not only prioritizes knowing and identifies knowledge with domination and mastery over the phenomena that are to be known but also insists on the metaphysical binarism that events must either be material or immaterial, physical or mental. The theories of 'psychoanalysis' are determinedly euromodern—committed to the conceptual expunction of psychic energy and thence mocking the praxis of listening free-associatively.

Thus, so much of the future of psychoanalysis pivots on whether the ontological composition of psychic reality might indeed be threefold: body, mind, *and* subtle energies that run within, through, and around the operations of both body and mind. Can we acknowledge and appreciate psychoanalysis as a discipline of healing the psyche that opens each individual's discourse to such forces as might be both material and immaterial, neither solely material nor solely immaterial?

This needs to be emphasized: That we cannot affirm the reality of psychic energies positively—that is, represent them, observe, or infer their operations rationally—cannot be assumed to imply that they do not exist and do not impact and influence us profoundly and pervasively.

Predictably, it will be objected that the thesis presented in this essay leads psychoanalysis towards being considered a practice of meditation and a discipline of mysticism. But unlike most methods of meditation, free-association does not claim to transcend the representational psyche, but rather to undo—dismantle or deconstruct—the blockages, inhibitions, and obstacles that it produces masking our capacity to be aware of subtle energies within and around our erotic embodiment. Obviously, there is something mystical about subtle energies, for the simple reason that they affect every aspect of our being-becoming, yet we cannot represent them in our thoughts, feelings, wishes, and fantasies. All we can gain by free-associative praxis is an illuminating sense of their mobilization or immobilization within us. Psychoanalysis is so thoroughly grounded in the lived-experiences of the patient and the psychoanalyst that this discipline is far from the province of the woo-woos. However, we cannot avoid the realization that, in the deathfulness and lifefulness of the ebb and flow of subtle energies within us, there is something deeply mysterious about the liveliness of life itself, and especially of the energetic interconnectedness of all beings.

We cannot avoid the conclusion that the radicalization of the free-associative method loosens the psychoanalytic subject's attachment to the secular challenges of interpretive understanding towards the possibility of listening to the dimension of the sacred. However, if one subscribes to an epistemology-first version of 'psychoanalysis'—believing that everything that exists must sooner or later be able to be apprehended and encapsulated in the rationality of representations and in our self-consciousness—then free-association is indeed still interesting, but rather unremarkable. The soft method is important simply as a diminution of censorship. However, if one concedes that there might be energetic forces that operate within both our material body and our immaterial mind, yet are identical to neither, then psychoanalysis diverges profoundly from what has, for over a century, passed as 'psychoanalysis.'

Free-association, as a radical praxis, undoes the obstacles and impediments to our being-becoming in a non-representational awareness of the movements of psychic energy. As Freud insisted, this mysterious method is the *since qua non* of psycho-*analysis.*

The prioritization of ontology over epistemology, the concern for being-becoming rather than the worries of knowing, did not get entirely expunged after 1914. For example, in the anglophone literature, one reads it implicitly in some of the field theories that have emerged in the wake of Bion's thinking about the cognitive functions that he called 'O' (not to be confused with the Lacanian upper-case Other) in some of the attitudes conveyed in Donald Winnicott's writings and those of his followers, and perhaps explicitly in Ogden's recent proclamations. By calling into question the valuation of the extant theoretical frameworks of 'psychoanalysis' and my investigating a radicalization of free-associative praxis, this essay has argued that *genuine psycho-analysis is an ontoethical discipline.*

Psycho-*analysis* is ontological in that it concerns the shifting momentum of our being-becoming and how we have to forego the enterprise of interpretation in order to learn listening-to-listen—the praxis that sharpens and amplifies our awareness but does not accrue to the expansion of our representational capacity. It is ethical in that it involves the opening of discourse to what *is*. As has been argued, such a process of opening—remobilizing our being-becoming—depends on the dismantling or deconstructing of the representational obstacles and impediments to the free flow of our being-becoming. That is precisely what radical free-association achieves in a way that, operating within our psychic reality, is uniquely precious.

Unlike the psychotherapeutic commitment to adaptation, the discipline of psycho-*analysis* is a praxis of freedom. But this is not freedom as a state that can be formulated. Philosophers have wrangled over that for many centuries. We cannot define freedom, but we can experience a *process of freeing*, an ecstatic (*ex-stasis*) release from that which blocks our awareness and the kinesis of our being-becoming. That is the free-associative process. The discipline of psycho-*analysis* is not an arrival at truths, as representational formulations that are correspondent with something outside of themselves, or that are rational, coherent, and pragmatically useful. In free-associative listening, we cannot define or arrive at truths like that, but we can experience a *process of truthfulness*. The praxis of truthfulness is liberation through the awareness of what *is*, the freeing of our being-becoming from the psychosomatic blocks we hold within us: Radical free-association as the ontoethical praxis of liberatory truthfulness.

Acknowledgements and Appreciations

The list of those who have contributed, over the years, to the development of my understanding of Freud's discipline is too long to inscribe here. In any event, it would have to include my patients, who must remain nameless (and there are many since I started doing psychoanalytic treatments 50 years ago). With apology and regret, I must limit my expression of appreciation to those individuals whose direct or indirect support—intellectual, emotional, or practical—felt particularly valuable to me during the specific period of this essay's production. In this regard, I gratefully acknowledge the following (in alphabetical order): Scharlene Dawn, Loray Daws, Jill Gentile, Lewis Gordon, Delia Hamlett, Jeremy Holmes, Cathrine Ngobeni, Jerry Piven, Lalita Salins, and Steven Sidley.

Recommendations for further reading

The understanding of psychoanalysis and its history that is argued in this essay is well represented on the website, www.rediscoveringpsychoanalysis.org, which offers many resources for reading and podcast listening. The following is a brief and highly selective list of additional recommendations for further study.

Barratt's writings most closely related to this essay

Barratt, BB (1984/2016). *Psychic Reality and Psychoanalytic Knowing*. London: Routledge. See also: *Psychoanalysis and the Postmodern Impulse: Knowing and Being since Freud's Psychology* (1993/2016). These two volumes comprise a serious effort to locate Freud's method in the context of euromodern and postmodern philosophies.

Barratt, BB (2016). *Radical Psychoanalysis: An Essay on Free-associative Praxis*. London: Routledge. The middle volume of the 'Rediscovering Psychoanalysis' trilogy (see also *What is Psychoanalysis?* and *Beyond Psychotherapy*) details at somewhat greater length the basic arguments presented in this essay.

Influential writings on free-association and related issues

Bollas, C (2002). *Free-Association: Ideas in Psychoanalysis*. Cambridge: Icon.

Bollas, C (2007). *The Freudian Moment*. London: Karnac.

Bollas, C (2009). *The Evocative Object World*. Hove: Routledge.

Bollas, C (2009). *The Infinite Question*. Hove: Routledge.

Bollas' commitment to free-association—as articulated in these volumes—has been of unparalleled significance in illustrating one dimension of the richness of this method.

Kris, AO (1996/2018). *Free Association: Method and Process* (revised and expanded edition). London: Routledge. This is Kris's landmark essay, which, at least briefly, kept alive an interest in free-association within the anglophone world.

Lombardi, G (2023). *The Clinical Method in the Analytic Perspective* (translated by A. Zorzutti). Lafayette, CO: Cuerno Verde Press. Written by one of South America's most eminent psychoanalysts, this is a useful exploration of free-association from a contemporary Lacanian perspective.

Nancy, J-L (2002/2007). *Listening* (translated by C. Mandell). New York: Fordham University Press. This is very helpful in rethinking the way we listen; it is worth reading in conjunction with Nancy's essays on touching and embodiment.

Thompson, MG (2004). *The Ethic of Honesty: The Fundamental Rule of Psychoanalysis.* New York: Rodopi (Contemporary Psychoanalytic Studies). This book argues forcefully how the commitment to free-association demands what is, effectively, a pledge of honesty. This book should be read by everyone on the path to becoming a psychoanalyst.

Index

For Product Safety Concerns and Information please contact our EU representative GPSR@taylorandfrancis.com Taylor & Francis Verlag GmbH, Kaufingerstraße 24, 80331 München, Germany

Printed and bound by CPI Group (UK) Ltd, Croydon, CR0 4YY
23/04/2026
02096043-0002